✿ THE FAIRY RING ✿

OR

Elsie and Frances Fool the World

Mary Losure

CANDLEWICK PRESS

First paperback edition 2014

Library of Congress Catalog Card Number 2011046081
ISBN 978-0-7636-5670-6 (hardcover)
ISBN 978-0-7636-7495-3 (paperback)

14 15 16 17 18 19 BVG 10 9 8 7 6 5 4 3 2 1

Printed in Berryville, VA, U.S.A.

This book was typeset in Mrs. Eaves.

Candlewick Press
99 Dover Street
Somerville, Massachusetts 02144

visit us at www.candlewick.com

To A.R.B.

Contents

✥

Part One ✦ FRANCES'S FAIRIES   I

1   Cottingley, Yorkshire, England   3

2   The Waterfall   8

3   Little Men   17

4   Black Box   26

5   One Glass Plate   33

6   Enter the Gnome   39

7   Frances Says Good-bye to Cottingley   43

Part Two ✦ ELSIE   51

8   A Letter from London   53

9   The Fairy Machine   61

10   Mr. Gardner Receives a Package   69

11   Mr. Gardner Persists   73

12   Spider Girl   81

13   Sincerely Yours, Elsie Wright   84

14   The Investigation   89

Part Three ❖ FRANCES AND ELSIE   101

15   Frances Comes for a Visit   103

16   An Epoch-Making Event   113

17   The Fairy Bower   123

18   The Glen Was Swarming   131

19   A Gentle See-through Fade-out   140

20   Fairy Grandmothers   149

21   Gorgeous and Precious Fairyland Places   160

Acknowledgments   167

Source Notes   169

Image Credits   178

Bibliography   179

Index   181

PART
ONE

Frances's Fairies

Cottingley, Yorkshire, England

For as long as she could remember, Frances's parents had told her stories about England. But when she got there, the real England wasn't like the stories at all. Frances could see that as soon as the ship pulled into the harbor.

It was only teatime, but night had already fallen. Frances had expected streetlamps and cheery windows with light showing through the curtains. Now all she could see was darkness.

It was something called a Blackout, Frances's parents said. It would last all night, every night, until the Great War was over.

Frances and her parents walked down the gangplank and through the dark, cold streets.

They boarded a train, and it rattled through the night. Sometimes it stopped and soldiers got off. More soldiers got on, with their guns and helmets and heavy packs.

When morning came, the train pulled into a small station. The sign on the platform said BINGLEY, and Frances knew that was their stop. Frances's father found a man with a horse and cart to take their trunks. He picked up the big leather suitcase that held their clothes.

Frances and her parents walked down Bingley's Main Street, past little shops and a church made of grim, gray stone.

It wasn't at all like the bustling streets of Cape Town, South Africa, where Frances had lived ever since she was a tiny baby. In Cape Town, her father wouldn't have had to lug a big heavy suitcase. They could have taken a taxicab.

Snow lay in drifts along the pavement. Frances picked some up and was surprised to find it was cold. Her parents laughed, but how was she to know? She'd only seen snow on Christmas cards, where it looked as white and soft as cotton.

They walked to the trolley stop and waited in the cold. When the trolley came, it was one of those glorious double-decker ones, so *that* at least was nice. They rode it through the winter-bare fields until it stopped at a bridge guarded by a big, round tower that looked like a castle. The conductor called out, "Cottingley Bar!"

Cottingley, Yorkshire, England, was where Frances and her mother would be staying for a while—nobody knew how long. They would live with Aunt Polly and Uncle Arthur and Cousin Elsie in their house in Cottingley while Frances's father was away in the War. He would be leaving for the battlefields in just two weeks.

A muddy lane led past a woolen mill that stank of grease and raw wool. Frances and her parents followed it up a hill, past a grand manor house, until they came to a village built of stone that seemed even grimmer and grayer than the streets of Bingley. Coal smoke rose from the chimneys into the cold air.

In Cape Town, the air smelled sweet and clear, like fir forests.

In Cape Town, women sold baskets of fragrant flowers that grew wild on the mountains.

Usually when Frances went places, she jumped and skipped and took the bottom four stairs at a bound. Usually she was always being told to "hush." But today her parents didn't have to tell her to walk quietly or hush.

They walked up the hill to the very edge of the village, and there stood a row of narrow houses all joined together. In the doorway of the very last one, Aunt Polly waited.

"Eeh!" she said, smiling widely. She had an odd sort of accent. A Yorkshire accent, Frances realized.

She was the most beautiful woman Frances had ever seen.

Her hair was the same color as Frances's mother's hair: shining brown with touches of auburn and gold. She wore a beautiful, old-fashioned green dress that went well with her hair.

Frances remembered that first meeting with her aunt for the rest of her life. But oddly enough, she couldn't remember the first time she met her cousin Elsie.

Memory is a funny thing sometimes. Maybe Frances didn't remember because Elsie . . . well, Elsie was the kind of person who seemed as though you'd always known her.

TWO

The Waterfall

Now that Frances lived at 31 Main Street, when she came home she opened the front gate and stepped through a tiny garden. It was shaped like a postage stamp, with a low fence all around it. It was the last in a line of postage-stamp gardens, one for each of the seven houses in the row.

The front door opened onto a small, formal parlor with flowered wallpaper. Lace curtains framed the room's one window, which looked out onto the muddy lane that was Main Street.

If Frances went through the parlor (taking care not to knock over one of the potted palms or bang into the piano), she came to the kitchen, which was even smaller than the parlor.

Stairs from the kitchen led down to the cellar. It was bright, for a cellar, with windows looking out to the back garden. A tin bathtub hung on the wall. The cellar door opened to the back garden, where a path led to the privy.

If Frances bounded back up the stairs, she came to the bedrooms: one for Elsie and one for Elsie's parents.

The top story was an attic, which had been made into another bedroom now that Frances's family was here.

Still, that made only three bedrooms for two sets of parents and Elsie and Frances. That meant the only place for Frances to sleep was in Elsie's room.

Elsie's room was so small that there was hardly space for one bed, let alone two. So Frances and Elsie shared a bed.

❋　❋　❋

It was lucky that Elsie didn't mind.

Elsie was much older—fifteen going on sixteen, while Frances was only nine. Elsie was a good head taller than Frances, too. Still, she was nice to Frances from the very beginning. Frances was glad, she wrote later, that her first friend in England would be her lighthearted cousin. Elsie had a "wide beaming smile" and beautiful, thick dark hair. She laughed a lot.

Elsie let Frances look at her watercolor paintings, which she kept in an old chocolate box under her bed. Sometimes she even played dolls with Frances.

Elsie's window looked out over the back garden, which sloped down to a little valley, its treetops bare now in the wintertime. A stream ran through it.

Elsie called it a *beck,* a Yorkshire word for stream. The beck was frozen now, but Elsie said in summer there was a waterfall.

One day, when Frances and her parents had been in Cottingley for two weeks, Frances's father packed his things and boarded the train for France. In France, he would be a gunner on the front lines.

Now each week when the newspaper came, it showed rows and rows of photographs of men and boys from Yorkshire who had volunteered to fight, just as Frances's father had. Next to each name were a few words saying what had happened to each soldier.

Killed.

Wounded.

Missing.

Sometimes the words were *shell shock, septic poisoning,* or *found in German trench.*

And every week, there would be a new batch of photographs.

Frances's mother's hair began to thin. The doctor said it was from worry. After a while, Frances's mother lost all her hair and wore a wig.

Soldiers in the War didn't get paid very much, so Frances's mother had to find a job. She went to work for Uncle Enoch. He had a tailor's shop in Bradford, which was a big city bristling with smokestacks from woolen mills.

Now, every workday, Frances's mother took the

Cottingley Village, painted by Elsie the summer she turned 15

trolley to Bradford and came home tired, wearing a wig made out of somebody else's old dead hair.

That spring when the snow melted and the beck thawed, Frances lay awake at night, staring at the black windowpanes and listening to the terrible roar of the rushing water.

In time, though, the roar faded to a pleasant murmur. Elsie said that when the banks dried out, they could go exploring in the beck.

On a warm, sunny Saturday, Elsie and Frances clattered down the kitchen stairs to the cellar. They opened the cellar door and followed the moss-covered stone path through the back garden. At the garden's edge, the path dropped steeply down.

All her life, Frances would remember that day, the "running water and the sun shining." The streambed, with its shallow pools and clear water swirling over dark rock, led up the valley and through the trees with their delicate spring leaves.

And the waterfall! It was just a few steps from where the garden path descended into the valley. There, the stream plunged downward over the rock into a lovely clear pool.

And it was right out Elsie's back door!

That spring, Frances and Elsie built dams, watched the water rise behind them, then broke the dams with a *whoosh.* They built tiny boats and floated them across the pools. They caught baby frogs and sailed them on the boats, watching to see whose frog would stay on longer.

From down in the beck, a few upstairs windows, almost hidden by the trees' new leaves, were all they could see of the world above. The cramped rooms of 31 Main Street, the grown-ups' comings and goings, and the life of the village seemed far away.

Often they just sat by the stream and talked.

Even though Elsie was taller and older, she seemed to understand what it was like for Frances to be a stranger in a strange place. She knew what it was like to be teased, too.

Both their fathers teased them.

Frances's father laughed at how she sang and

danced when she was little. He criticized the mistakes Frances made in her letters to him.

Elsie's father teased her that in school—where the bad students sat on one side of the aisle and the good students sat on the other—Elsie was "the best among the worst," or sometimes "the worst among the best."

Elsie's father himself was so smart he could fix any kind of machine, including all the latest motorcars. He could sing wonderfully and play the piano. He loved to read.

Elsie couldn't sing *or* play the piano. She was a slow reader, a terrible speller, and was always getting scolded for daydreaming.

In school Elsie had hated every single subject except drawing and painting. So she had quit! She had left the village school when she was thirteen and a half, the youngest age the law allowed. Now that she was fifteen, she worked in Bradford at a boring job. But she still loved to paint.

Frances thought her paintings were wonderful.

❀ ❀ ❀

So that was Elsie, Frances's first friend in England. She loved a good laugh, she loved to paint, and she didn't like being teased.

Those things were the key to everything that happened later.

But neither of them knew that yet.

THREE

Little Men

Now that the weather was nice, Frances walked home from school instead of taking the trolley. She went to an expensive school in Bingley because it was better than the village school in Cottingley.

Her school friends were all in Bingley. So every day, by the time she got to Cottingley, she'd be walking all by herself.

If the village children were outside playing, they could stare at Frances as she hurried past in her uniform, her school hat with a ribbon, and her good leather school shoes. The village children went to school in their ordinary working clothes. Some of them wore wooden clogs.

If they said anything to her, it was in a Yorkshire accent so thick that it was almost another language.

Frances's parents had forbidden her to speak broad Yorkshire, but she tried to anyway. She left the *h* off the beginning of words like *had.* She began saying *me* for *my.*

The village children weren't fooled. Their school was only a few doors down from Frances's house, but for all the friends she made there, it might have been on the moon.

Every day when Frances pushed open the door at 31 Main Street, Elsie would be in Bradford, working. Frances would rush through her homework. Then she'd go down, all alone, to the beck.

She liked to catch frogs and study their bulging eyes. She liked to see their tiny throats going in and out and to feel their pointy fingers on her palm before they leaped away.

She liked to go exploring, following the stream up the little valley.

Huge, gnarled trees, their roots and trunks above her head, grew on the tops of the banks. Light slanted down, playing on spiderwebs and specks of floating dust.

She had her favorite tree now, in the beck. It was a willow leaning out over the water.

One day when the air was very still, Frances was sitting in her willow tree when she noticed a leaf moving, all by itself. There was no breeze, yet the leaf seemed to be twirling anyway. It was odd, but Frances didn't give it much thought until another afternoon, when the same thing happened: one leaf began to twirl.

All by itself.

As she peered through the willow branches, Frances noticed a little man. She described him, years later, in a book she wrote about her life. He was about eighteen inches high, dressed all in green, twiddling a willow leaf as he walked along the bank.

She wasn't all that surprised to see him, she wrote in her autobiography, and there being a little man there did explain the puzzle of the twirling leaf.

Truly, the beck was an extraordinary place.

A pair of rubber boots would have been useful for exploring, for then Frances could have waded through the shallow pools. Instead, she had to scramble over the slippery, moss-covered rocks in her one pair of leather shoes. She had to wear a dress, of course, since girls in those days did not wear pants, and it was hard to keep the hem dry. When she came home wet and muddy, she got in trouble, but how could anyone stay away from a place like the beck?

She sat by the stream for hours, watching the little men.

Once, one of them broke off a willow branch without the least effort.

Frances was surprised. After all, the stems and leaves of trees are usually tough. Most people have to give them a good tug to pull them off.

Frances watched as, twirling the leaf, the little man

walked down the bank and crossed the stream, right on top of the water.

He had a rugged face like the workingmen at the railway station who drove carts pulled by huge, beautiful workhorses. He wore a serious expression, as though he had a job to do.

One day Frances saw him leading a crew of three or four other little men. All were dressed in green coats and baggy tights in a darker shade of green. They marched down the bank, crossed the beck, and turned right. Frances watched them until they went behind a clump of willow herb and were gone.

A few weeks after she spotted the little men, Frances saw some other fairies: the flitting, winged kind that many people think of when they hear the word *fairy*. Their dresses were wishy-washy pastels. Frances liked the little men better.

The pastel fairies seemed to have a lot of meetings, though, and every once in a while a dark-blue, take-charge, no-nonsense fairy would show up. She reminded Frances of a Head Prefect at school.

Once, the fairies held a very big meeting. It was like something she'd been learning about in school called a wapentake. *Wapentake* is an ancient Viking word for a "weapon take," where all the chiefs meet and hand over their weapons. Frances wondered what the fairies were doing at their meeting. Were they counting heads, conducting a census of some kind? Or maybe they were holding an election?

She wondered how the fairies communicated, for she never heard them speak or saw their mouths move. Sometimes she heard a high-pitched sound, like a ringing in her ears.

Frances never tried to talk to them. She just observed them quietly and carefully, the way a scientist would.

They never paid any attention to her, but still, she thought they could see her. After all, the first time she'd seen a little man—the one who was all by himself—he'd given her a good hard stare before he went on his way.

❀ ❀ ❀

For a long time, Frances never told anyone, not even Elsie.

Sometimes when Frances and Elsie were in the beck together, Frances saw the fairies. But Elsie never said anything about them! Not even when the fairies were quite near.

After a while, Frances did tell Elsie.

After all, Elsie wasn't the kind of person who would laugh at you for seeing fairies.

One night after a long day at work, Frances's mother opened the front door and stepped though the tiny sitting room into the kitchen. There on the linoleum was a big, muddy puddle.

In her whole life, Frances's mother had never yelled at her, but she did that night. *Why* couldn't Frances stay out of the beck? She'd never been disobedient before! *What* was she going to do with her? Besides, there was nothing in the beck, anyway!

And Frances (for the first time in *her* life) yelled at her mother. "There is! I go up to see the fairies!"

Frances's mother stared. The kitchen was dead silent.

"That's the end," said Aunt Polly. "You've started telling stories now!"

Aunt Polly turned to Elsie and asked her if she'd seen any fairies.

Elsie stood right next to Frances and said yes, she had.

By then, Uncle Arthur had come into the kitchen, but he didn't say a word.

In the silence, Frances's mother went upstairs to take off her coat and hat. Aunt Polly finished making tea.

They all sat down at the kitchen table.

None of them said much, because nobody seemed to know what to say.

Later, none of the grown-ups asked Frances anything more about the beck. Instead, if Frances was late coming home from one of her piano lessons, they'd ask her if she'd seen any fairies lately.

They teased Elsie, too, if she went into one of her daydreams. Maybe *she'd* seen some fairies?

Pretty soon Elsie said she was sick of it. And then . . . she told Frances she had an idea.

Why not take a photograph of the fairies? It would stop the teasing once and for all.

It would be splendid.

FOUR

Black Box

Elsie would borrow her father's camera, she said. She'd never taken a photograph in her life, but that didn't seem to stop her.

It was summer now, and Elsie's father had just gotten his first camera, secondhand from Uncle Percy. It was a wooden box about nine inches tall, covered with pebble-textured black paper. It had a leather strap on top. It weighed about two and a half pounds.

It didn't use the kind of film that came in rolls, which was a rather recent American invention.

Instead, Elsie's father's London-made camera used an old-fashioned kind of film that came mounted on glass plates. "Perhaps the advent of the luxurious roll-film has, to a certain extent, displaced the box-plate camera from its proud position of constant companion," the camera's instruction manual admitted. "But," it added, "there is no gainsaying the fact that the best pictures have always been, and will always be, produced from plates." Each photograph taken with Elsie's father's camera required its own glass plate.

To load the plates into the camera, you had to take it into a darkroom, "i.e. a room from which all light, except that given by a ruby lamp . . . has been excluded," according to the manual. Elsie's father had built his own darkroom in a tiny space in the cellar, tucked under the stairs that came down from the kitchen. He didn't have a ruby lamp. Instead, he had blocked off the darkroom's one window except for a small pane of red glass.

In the dim red light of the darkroom, you had to insert the plates, one by one, into metal holders known as sheaths, taking care to make sure the film side of the glass plates was facing up. You had to load each sheath into the camera, then close the camera's hinged door, which had a large spring that held the sheaths in place.

Just recently, Elsie's father had begun taking his first photos. Anyone could see by watching him that it wasn't easy.

First (by working a lever on the front of the camera) he had to adjust the amount of light that went into the lens. Too much light, and the picture would be washed out. Too little, and it would be too dark.

He also had to set the shutter speed, again using a lever on the front of the camera.

He had to stand the right distance from whatever he was photographing (a distance that depended on the setting he'd chosen for the light) and decide which of the two glass viewfinders he wanted to use: the one on the side of the box or the one on top. And finally, he had to work the shutter (another lever, on the side of the box) very carefully. "A steady pressure should be maintained on the lever until the shutter is released," the manual warned, as "a jerky, sudden movement will seriously affect the ultimate picture."

But Elsie's father's photographs turned out wonderfully.

One of them showed tall Elsie and a much shorter Frances. They were standing side by side in the sunshine by the beck in their bathing costumes.

It was a good thing the pictures turned out so well, since each glass plate cost quite a bit of money.

One Wednesday night, Uncle Arthur and Aunt Polly went off to choir practice and Frances and her mother went to Bradford to visit Aunt Clara. When Frances got home and she and Elsie were alone in their room, Elsie said she had something to show her.

It was a set of beautifully painted cutout paper fairies.

Elsie had copied the bodies from some dancing fairies in one of Frances's storybooks, then added bigger wings. She had cut them out so carefully that not one tiny sliver of paper showed around the edges.

Frances was filled with admiration.

Elsie slipped them into a book and hid it under her bed.

Now all she needed was some hatpins (the long, sharp pins ladies used to fasten their big hats to their high-piled hair) and some gum, for attaching the cutouts to the hatpins.

Then, when the cutouts, the hatpins, and the gum were all ready, Elsie and Frances would wait for the next time the grown-ups asked them if they'd seen any fairies lately.

It was a bright, sunny July day when someone made the next fairy remark.

Quick as anything, Elsie told her father that if he'd lend her his camera, she'd take the fairies' picture.

It was only fair, she said. He should either lend her the camera or stop teasing.

Uncle Arthur didn't like the idea one bit, but

The dancing fairies in Frances's storybook

Elsie and Frances pestered him. Nattered him, as Elsie would say in her Yorkshire way.

Aunt Polly and Frances's mother laughed and took the girls' side, and finally, after much grumbling, Uncle Arthur went down to his darkroom and returned with the camera. He gave it to Elsie and told her she had to carry it, not Frances. "There's one plate in. If you make a mess of it you won't get another," he said, "and mind you take care of my camera."

Then, with Uncle Arthur yelling, "Now take care!" behind them, Elsie and Frances raced for the beck.

FIVE

One Glass Plate

At the little pool at the bottom of the waterfall, Frances took her shoes off and waded. Elsie wandered around, looking at all the sunny spots nearby. In a little while, she called Frances over.

Elsie had stuck the hatpins, each with its dancing fairy, on a mossy bank among a tangle of ferns and wildflowers.

The watercolor fairies danced barefoot, on tiptoe, their filmy dresses and long hair flying. Elsie had painted their wings with spots like butterflies' wings. One fairy played a set of long pipes. They were graceful, cheery-looking little creatures, with beautiful slender ankles.

Frances told Elsie how pretty they were. Then she got down behind them.

Frances was wearing an everyday dress with the sleeves rolled up, but the wreath of pansies in her hair looked nice. She rested her chin on her hand and gazed at the camera.

Elsie held the black box, Frances watched, and Elsie pressed the lever.

After that, the two girls tore the paper fairies into little tiny pieces. They stuck the hatpins deep into the earth, climbed out of the beck, and gave the camera back to Uncle Arthur.

There wasn't room for three in the darkroom, so Elsie and her father crowded into the little space under the stairs while Frances waited outside the door. There in the cellar, with the bright garden just outside, Frances hopped and jumped and danced in anticipation.

And then, from behind the darkroom door, she heard Elsie yell.

The fairies were on the plate!

Uncle Arthur wasn't at all pleased, to hear Elsie tell it later. At first, as they watched the image emerge from the tray of darkroom chemicals, he grumbled that it was a nice picture of Frances, but they'd messed it up by leaving trash from a picnic lying around. He thought the fairies' wings were "sandwich papers," Elsie said, until he saw all the little legs coming up.

Uncle Arthur asked Elsie how she did it, but Elsie wouldn't say. Later, in secret, she made Frances promise not to say anything, either.

Frances never heard the grown-ups discussing the photograph or the fairies, but now, at least, they didn't fuss when she went down to the beck.

Maybe they figured she'd need new school shoes next year anyway? Or maybe it was that she had learned to keep her footing better on the rocks?

But whatever their reasons were, the grown-ups left Frances in peace.

Down in the beck, the little men came and went, walking up and down the streambed in single file. Frances got to know their comings and goings: they reminded her of people going to work on a train every day. She especially liked to watch her favorite little man, the one who was always last in line. He wasn't as serious as the rest of them. Every once in a while, as he brought up the rear, he'd hop or skip or do a little jig.

On fine summer mornings when Frances woke up, other sounds besides the brook might drift through her window: horses' hooves in the lane, the clack of the mowing machines, the bleating of sheep in the fields. And in time, there were other things to do besides going down, all alone, to the beck.

When haymaking season came, Frances and Aunt Polly volunteered to help a farmer named Mr. Snowden. His farm lay right at the edge of Cottingley Village, not far from 31 Main Street. He needed

Frances and the fairies

help with his hay because so many men were away in the War.

With pitchforks, Frances and Aunt Polly tossed the hay into the wagon. Then they got to climb up and ride on top of the load. They would lie in the sweet-smelling hay while Mr. Snowden drove down the country lanes, past hedges blooming with roses and honeysuckle.

Mr. Snowden had a daughter named Ada, and she and Frances became friends. After that, Frances often went to visit her at Manor Farm.

Ada wasn't silent like the little men.

Frances and Ada would climb to the top of the haystack and sit there for hours, just talking.

SIX

Enter the Gnome

L ate that summer, Frances and Elsie's cousin Judith got married. Frances and Elsie both got to be in the wedding. They wore white dresses their mothers made for them.

Elsie's father took pictures of the wedding party for the family photo album. Visitors always liked to look at it. The photo of Frances and the fairies wasn't included, but Frances and Elsie and Aunt Polly liked to take the fairy picture out of its drawer and show it to people anyway.

No one ever knew what to make of it, but they often gushed about how lovely the fairies were.

Then one day, Elsie told Frances she wanted to take another photograph. She had already picked a spot for it when, on a sunny Saturday in September, she talked Uncle Arthur into lending her the camera. He loaded it with one plate, just as he had before.

Elsie put on the flowing white dress she'd worn to Cousin Judith's wedding, then she and Frances set off for the beck. In her long skirt, Elsie followed the path down to the streambed and picked her way among the rocks and pools. After a while, she climbed up the stream bank to a field dotted with huge oak trees.

When she got to the right spot, she stuck a paper cutout (gummed to a hatpin) into the soft ground.

The figure she'd painted this time had a beard, a pointy hat, long spindly legs, and a sly expression. From its back sprouted what looked like wings. The gnome—for so it was—appeared to be tiptoeing across the grass.

Elsie checked to see that all the levers on the camera were set correctly. She selected a place that was the right distance from the gnome, then set the camera carefully on the ground.

Frances got down near the camera.

Elsie sat behind the gnome and arranged her skirts gracefully around her ankles. Over her long dark hair, she wore a shapeless, wide-brimmed gnomish sort of hat that went nicely with the gnome itself.

Then Elsie extended her fingertips so that they grazed the gnome's little paper hand. She smiled at the little man, as though they were just now meeting in the woods. At that exact moment, Frances took the picture.

She pressed the little lever, and *click!* It was done.

After that, Elsie took the camera back so Uncle Arthur could develop the plate. Frances stayed in the beck to play.

At teatime, when Frances came home, the picture was set out to dry, but Frances didn't pay much attention to it.

After all, it was only a paper fairy.

Elsie and the gnome

~

SEVEN

Frances Says Good-bye to Cottingley

Fall and winter passed, and then another summer. Frances still saw fairies in the beck, but now their lives seemed rather aimless. "Fairies—the pretty, pretty ones—are just fairies," Frances wrote, "and there's not much I can say about them."

Frances's father came home on leave, with his big pack and his tin hat hanging by a strap from his shoulder. Then, a week later, he had to return to France, for the war was still not over.

Frances wrote a letter to her friend Joanna in South Africa.

Dear Joe,

I hope you are quite well. I wrote a letter before, only I lost it or it got mislaid. Do you play with Elsie and Nora Biddles? I am learning French, Geometry, Cookery and Algebra at school now. Dad came home from France the other week . . . and we all think the War will be over in a few days. We are going to get our flags to hang upstairs in our bedroom. I am sending two photos, both of me, one of me in a bathing costume in our back yard. Uncle Arthur took that, while the other is me with some fairies up the beck, Elsie took that one. Rosebud is as fat as ever and I have made her some new clothes. How are Teddy and Dolly?

On the back of the fairy photograph, Frances wrote, *Elsie and I are very friendly with the beck fairies. It is funny I never used to see them in Africa. It must be too hot for them there.*

One day in November, the teachers at Frances's school called an assembly just before lunchtime.

It seemed an odd time for an assembly, and when Frances got there, the teachers were all wearing their caps and gowns.

Then someone made an announcement:

The War was over!

School was let out!

Frances and all the other children sang "God Save the King" and gave three cheers. Then she and all her friends went running down the corridors and didn't even get in trouble. Outside on the streets of Bingley, grown-ups were pouring out of the offices and mills, singing and shouting.

When Frances got to Cottingley, the mill hooters were sounding. People were hanging flags out their upstairs windows. Elsie came home early from Bradford, and Frances's mother did, too.

That night, for the first time since Frances had come to Cottingley, the houses in the village were all lit up, their blinds drawn and the windowpanes shining. The Blackout was over! People were spilling out into the streets.

But at 31 Main Street, Uncle Arthur sat in his

armchair, reading a book. *He* wasn't going anywhere that night—and he said no one else was, either.

The sounds of people singing drifted into the cramped parlor. Footsteps in wooden clogs clattered on the cobblestones outside. Frances and Elsie grumbled as much as they dared, but it did no good.

Someone came to the door and said the trolley cars to Bradford were so crammed full that you could ride for free and people were riding outside on the trolley steps as everyone cheered and sang and waved flags. . . .

Frances almost cried.

The next day at school, all the girls talked about how their parents had taken them out for that wonderful night, and Frances knew she had missed what would have been one of the greatest moments of her life.

Because of Uncle Arthur.

But still . . . the War was over! And although Frances's father was still a soldier and wouldn't be coming home quite yet, he was alive, and that was what mattered. Frances and her mother sent him a parcel of books for his Christmas present in France.

That year when spring came, Frances noticed how beautiful England was—not just in the beck but everywhere. Running home from school in Bingley, she looked up and saw the tiny new tree leaves against the pale spring sky, and the world was a wonderful place.

When the beck thawed, the little men were still there. Frances noticed that they seemed to be wearing a paler shade of green than they had last year. "My little friend, the one always last in the file, was just as enchantingly childish. They still took no notice of me but I felt I was amongst friends now," Frances wrote years later in her autobiography.

That fall, right after Frances's twelfth birthday, she and her mother moved away from Cottingley to a seaside town called Scarborough. Her father, who was out of the army now, would be joining them soon.

There were no fairies in Scarborough, but there

were ocean waves and sandy beaches, just like in South Africa. On sunny days the water was a beautiful blue.

Frances loved the big, ornate old hotels down by the water. She loved the little lonely coves with slopes of sea grass and cliffs covered with wildflowers.

She liked watching the fleets of wooden boats out fishing for herring, and the fishermen's wives who clicked away with their knitting needles as they walked around town, talking and looking in the shop windows.

One Tuesday, a month before Easter, Frances and her new friends from school ran down to the beach to watch a curious old custom, something people in Scarborough had done on that day ever since anyone could remember. Men at each end of long clothes-lines twirled them around and around, just as children do playing jump rope. Then everyone—not just children but fishermen, fishermen's wives, shop clerks, and even the most staid and sober of men—skipped rope on the sand.

Frances thought it was one of the nicest things she'd ever seen.

As for the fairies—who could say if she'd ever see them again?

Fairies come, and fairies go.

PART
TWO

Elsie

EIGHT

A Letter from London

In Elsie's house, the fairy photographs lay hidden away in a drawer.

Elsie had her room to herself now, with Frances gone. When the moon shone, the view was especially beautiful. The wind made a musical sound as it blew round the corner of the house, high on its hill.

Elsie was eighteen now, with her whole life ahead of her. Someday, she hoped to become an artist.

Once, in a photography shop window in Bradford, Elsie had seen some lovely portraits of children. They were black-and-white photographs, but somebody had colored them in by hand. And next to the portraits was a help-wanted notice.

So Elsie opened the shop door and went inside.

She got the job. But she soon found out it wasn't coloring in portraits.

Instead, she had to sit in the basement, in a long row of other girls, dabbing black paint on white specks where photographs hadn't come out quite right. The other girls were "school-leavers," just like her.

Mr. Gunston, the photographer, was too important to pay any attention to any of them. Sometimes Mr. Gunston's wife had Elsie run errands, and at least that was less boring than dabbing paint.

It was a "below the stairs" job—that's all.

So not too long after that, Elsie found another help-wanted notice. This one was in the newspaper, seeking young school-leavers with "artistic ability."

Elsie went to the address listed in the advertisement and found it was a button factory. She followed the manager to a back room. There, she saw two young girls sitting at easels, rubbing colored powder onto black-and-white photographs.

Many of the photographs were portraits of young men who had died in the War. A note attached to each photograph told what color the dead boy's eyes and hair had been.

It was sad, looking at so many boys who had been just about her age when they died. But at least it was better than the other job. It was closer to being a real artist.

At home, Elsie's drawings and paintings hung on the walls.

One was a watercolor of Cottingley Village, seen from the top of the hill. Elsie had painted the hay fields and Manor Farm and the lane down the hill. Above, she painted the wide sky and the birds winging away.

Sometimes Elsie drew gardens in faraway countries.

Once, she drew Titania, the queen of the fairies from Shakespeare's *A Midsummer Night's Dream.* The fairy

The Fairy Queen, copied by Elsie from an illustration by Arthur Rackham

queen lay sleeping on a bank, her lovely dark hair spread all around her.

Elsie had copied her out of a book illustrated by Arthur Rackham. Arthur Rackham was a real artist, famous for his illustrations of fairies.

But Elsie's own fairies—the dancing ones that everyone said were so beautiful—were torn up and buried in the beck. The painted paper gnome was long gone. Their photographs lay forgotten in a drawer. For all Elsie knew, no one would ever look at them again.

And maybe that's what would have happened if, one winter day, Elsie's mother hadn't decided to go on an outing. . . .

Elsie's mother went to Bradford, where she liked to go to the moving picture shows. Sometimes, when there wasn't anything she wanted to see at the cinema, she went to hear speakers of one kind or another.

That day she found herself in a square near the train station. In front of a grand stone building called Unity Hall, someone had posted a notice about a lecture on nature spirits. Elsie's mother went in.

Inside were hundreds and hundreds of seats, for the lectures in Unity Hall were very popular.

The speaker was from an organization of people known as Theosophists.

The Theosophists, it seemed, had all kinds of scientific theories about nature spirits. Elsie's mother listened closely. And nature spirits, it became clear as the talk went on, were . . . fairies.

The Theosophists didn't seem to think fairies were a joke at all. When the talk was over, Elsie's mother turned to the woman sitting next to her. Her daughter had taken a photograph of fairies, Elsie's mother said, but "we all thought they were nothing but mischievous nonsense!"

Someone hurried up to tell the lecturer. The next thing Elsie's mother knew, the Theosophists had arranged for a print of the photo of Frances and the fairy ring to be sent to London, where the English branch of the Theosophical Society had its headquarters.

Not long after that, a letter arrived for Elsie's mother.

It had been written on a typewriter, on stationery engraved with an address on the outskirts of London: 5 Craven Road, Harlesden, NW 10. Telephone: Willesden 1081. It was dated February 23, 1920.

Dear Mrs. Wright,

I have just seen a photograph of "Pixies" that [my friend] *Mrs. Powell has, and she tells me it is through your little girl that it was obtained.*

I am very anxious to make a collection of slides of such photographs for the Society's work and am writing to ask if you can very kindly assist me. The print I have seen is certainly the best of its kind I should think anywhere, and if you can help further I should be very greatly obliged. Perhaps you would be so kind as to answer the following queries presuming you have no objection. Of course when showing the pictures no names need be mentioned if desired.

1.   Circumstances under which this photo was taken. Situation? Is the girl seated behind a bank? Did the girl who took the photo see the pixies? Time of day? Date?

2.   Have you any other photographs of similar kind?

3.   Is it possible for me to have the negatives on loan for a week that I may prepare lantern slides?

4.   Do you think it feasible to attempt to take more of these? If so most gladly I would send all the plates necessary for the attempt and help in any way I can that you may suggest.

I am keenly interested in this side of our wonderful world life and am urging a better understanding of nature spirits and fairies. It will assist greatly if I was able to show actual photographs of some of the orders. Of course I know this can only be done by the help of children at present and am delighted to get into touch with such promising assistance as it seems your little girl can render.

Very sincerely yours,

Edward Gardner

NINE

The Fairy Machine

When Elsie's mother told her about the letter from London—written with a typewriter! from a man who belonged to an organization with branches all over the world!—Elsie could have told her mother and father the secret of the cutouts right then.

Elsie's mother would have had to write back to Mr. Gardner saying it had all been a big mistake. The fairies weren't real. They were only mischievous nonsense, after all, and that would have been the end of it.

But Elsie didn't tell.

She had no way of knowing it was a decision that would change her whole life.

But then, there were a lot of things Elsie didn't know.

How was *she* supposed to know that she had taken her photographs at a time when a number of very respectable, well-educated city people were starting to think that maybe fairies weren't "magic" at all?

Maybe, these people thought, fairies were just something science didn't understand yet but would soon. After all, many things seemed like magic if you didn't understand them. Telegraphs that sent messages through wires! X-rays that could see the bones inside your hand!

To some, it seemed quite likely that a camera could take pictures of fairies. After all, an X-ray could take pictures of things people couldn't see. Why couldn't a camera?

In discussions going on in faraway London, people suggested that maybe soon, scientists would be able to study fairies. Soon, they reasoned, fairies, hobgoblins, brownies, and so on could be sorted into scientific groups such as order, genus, and species.

And that—though Elsie had no way of knowing this—was why Mr. Gardner's letter asked Elsie to take "actual photographs of some of the orders."

It was as though by taking the fairy photographs, she had pushed a button on a huge machine. She had no way of understanding all its cogs and gears. But now, it was beginning to clank and whir.

And it wanted, very much, to find out more about fairies.

The fairy seekers knew certain things already, from fairy lore.

They knew that fairies could be tiny, or they could be the size of humans. Fairies often dressed in green. They feared iron. If you followed them into a fairy hill and ate their food, you might stay there for what seemed only a short while, but when you went home, you'd discover that your family and friends were dead and forgotten. Fairies stole human babies and left little wizened fairy creatures, called changelings, in the babies' cradles. Brownies helped around the house, especially if you left them a dish of milk.

Fairies often lived in valleys known as fairy glens. In modern times, fairies were retreating to wild places far from smoke and noise and machines. They lingered, still, in unspoiled countryside. And there (according to the experts in London), fairies could still be glimpsed by simple country folk.

And now . . . here was a report of a fairy sighting from . . . Yorkshire!

Hum, whir . . .

Yorkshire, with its heather-covered moors, was one of the wildest places in England.

Bing!

And two little country girls had spotted the fairies, which made sense, since country people were the ones who knew the most about fairies.

Clank, hum, whir . . .

Ireland, according to fairy experts, was an even better place to look for fairies than Yorkshire. Which was

Dancing fairies by Arthur Rackham, 1908

no doubt why Mr. Gardner's next letter began the way it did.

March 2nd [19]20

Dear Mrs. Wright,

Very many thanks indeed for your kind letter just received. If I may beg you to favour me so far do you think you could arrange with Miss Elsie to attempt some photographs of fairies in Ireland?

But now, what were Elsie and her mother supposed to say to the man from London?

The letter went on:

Should she not already be possessed of a camera I will very gladly send her a good hand Kodak or other make and a parcel of plates. If she has a choice of cameras please let me know which she likes best.

May I explain that I am responsible for the department of the Theosophical Society concerned with diagrams, lantern slides, &c., and have been for long anxious to obtain a few photographs of fairies, pixies, and elves, and if possible of brownies & goblins. The print I have from Mrs. Powell is the most beautiful and promising that I have ever seen and if I can enlist Miss Elsie's good services we may be able to get some really good ones and indeed a valuable collection. Please assure her that any stipulation she likes to impose by way of reserve, such as not mentioning names, &c., I will of course observe and am willing to assist so far as I can in any way she may think of.

I know quite well that fairies exist and that they are very shy of showing themselves or approaching adults, and it is only when one can obtain the help of their "friends" that one can hope to obtain photographs and hence lead to a better understanding of Nature's ways than is possible otherwise. So I am very anxious to secure this fine opportunity of assistance if you can very kindly help. Why not ask Miss Elsie to try for further photos in Yorkshire? Do, if you can! I will forward camera at once if necessary. I would suggest that her friend goes with her as I think a good deal of help is afforded by way of intensifying the fairies bodies by proximity, but this may not be necessary.

Is it possible for me to have the loan of the two negatives you speak of? I have only one of the prints and would have preferred the negatives for conversion if permitted. I would return them within a week. If not, may I have a print of the second photo, the one with the single "goblin"?

Sincerely yours,

Edward Gardner

TEN

Mr. Gardner
Receives a Package

In Harlesden, on the outskirts of London, Mr. Gardner opened a small cardboard box. Inside, there was a note from Elsie's mother and two glass plates. And there on the plates were the silvery outlines of two girls . . . fairy wings . . . and a small and curious creature.

Mr. Gardner hurried to the telephone and arranged with a photographer to have some prints made from the plates. Then he got on his bicycle and pedaled over to the nearby town of Harrow, where the photographer had his studio.

The road took him past newly built houses and factories, for the town where Mr. Gardner lived was rapidly being swallowed up by sooty, noisy London. Harrow, where the photographer's studio was, lay farther away from the city, so soon Mr. Gardner was pedaling through the pleasant countryside.

Anyone looking at him as he rode by would have seen a perfectly ordinary-looking man. True, he believed in fairies and unseen spirits—his sister had once considered him "bathed in error and almost past praying for"—but he wasn't a wild-eyed, wild-haired sort of person. He was a quiet, reserved man with short brown hair, a neatly trimmed brown beard, a brown suit, and a bow tie.

Mr. Gardner cycled past fields and woods till the town of Harrow appeared in the distance. When he reached the photographer's studio, he climbed down from his bicycle and went inside.

He handed the plates to Mr. Snelling, the photographer. Mr. Snelling took them over to a glass-topped desk. He flipped on an electric light underneath the glass, took out a magnifying lens, and peered at the plates.

He looked at them for a long, long time.

April 8th, [19]20

Dear Mrs. Wright,

With very many thanks indeed I am returning the two negatives Miss Elsie so kindly sent me. . . . I think it might interest you and her to know that when I set about obtaining some prints from them I took them to one of the best experts in photography in London and without describing the negatives at all asked him if he would make me some prints.

He looked at the first negative (the one with several) and exclaimed and then carefully examined it further and then said "this is the most extraordinary photograph I have ever seen!" I wanted to hear exactly what he thought so simply asked him why. He said "because there appear to be some dancing fairy figures on the plate and the photograph is a straightforward genuine one!" I then asked him bluntly whether the negative could have been built up by any faking. . . . He laughed when he said that had the plate been a faked one it would not have interested him at all, he was accustomed to handling and making up faked photographs constantly, but to him the amazing thing was that this plate was not faked, but was absolutely genuine!

I was myself convinced the photograph was quite genuine from the start, as I told you, but it was very interesting to have this testimony from an expert London photographer accustomed to dealing with thousands of films of every sort in his business. . . .

Please let me know if Miss Elsie can be persuaded to attempt to take some more. I shall be immensely indebted to her if she will and will despatch the camera and plates . . . [as soon as] I hear. Pray tell her that she will be doing a real service in doing this if she will, more perhaps than she imagines. We want to learn something further about the fairy world and the very best way will be by photographs if only we can obtain them.

Very sincerely yours,
Edward Gardner

ELEVEN

Mr. Gardner Persists

Four days later, the mailman brought something else — a box of chocolates and a letter addressed to Miss Elsie Wright.

"I am myself convinced of fairies — have been all my life, but the best photograph I have ever seen is undoubtedly yours," Mr. Gardner wrote.

The subject is quite an important one and you would be doing us all a considerable service if you could get further photographs of a similar kind of the various varieties. I will most willingly assist in every way possible. . . . Many of us wish to learn more about this delightful side of life and if you can help I shall be immensely grateful. Will you think of it and let me know?

It was Elsie's mother who wrote Mr. Gardner back.

She could have explained that Elsie was a terrible speller who hardly ever wrote letters. But Elsie's mother was nice enough not to.

Instead, she said that she was writing for her daughter because Elsie was sick:

"She says I must thank you ever so many times, indeed it was very kind of you, but she does not know if she can take any more," Elsie's mother wrote.

The little niece of mine from South Africa, the one on the picture [h]as gone away. If she does take any more I will send them on. Thank you very much for the offer of the camera but we have two, and her dad lets her have the use of them now.

Yours Sincerely,
Polly Wright

Now what?

Mr. Gardner had sent a box of chocolates and a letter for Elsie, not her mother.

He did not seem to be going away.

And far away in London, the fairy machine was rolling onward.

In London, Mr. Gardner had had lantern slides made from the two glass plates. Now he was showing the pictures of Frances and the fairies and Elsie and the gnome on screens at auditoriums all over town. Every day, more and more people heard about the fairy photographs.

One of them was a writer who was conducting his own research on fairies. He planned to publish an article—with firsthand accounts of actual fairy sightings—in one of England's most popular illustrated magazines, the *Strand*.

And they did make fascinating reading.

In one account, a man called Mr. Lonsdale described the fairies that he and his friend Mr. Turvey had seen in Mr. Turvey's garden.

We sat in a hut which had an open front looking on to the lawn. We had been perfectly quiet for some time, neither talking nor moving, as was often our habit. Suddenly I was conscious of a movement on the edge of the lawn, which on that side went up to a grove of pine trees. Looking closely, I saw several little figures dressed in brown peering through the bushes. They remained quiet for a few minutes and then disappeared. In a few seconds a dozen or more small people, about two feet in height, in bright clothes and with radiant faces, ran on to the lawn, dancing hither and thither. I glanced at Turvey to see if he saw anything, and whispered, "Do you see them?" He nodded. These fairies played about, gradually approaching the hut. One little fellow, bolder than the others, came to a croquet hoop close to the hut and, using the hoop as a horizontal bar, turned round and round it, much to our amusement. Some of the others watched him, while others danced about, not in any set dance, but seemingly moving in sheer joy. This continued for four or five minutes, when suddenly, evidently in response to some signal or warning from those dressed in brown, who had remained at the edge of the lawn, they all ran into the wood. Just then a maid appeared coming from the house with tea. Never was tea so unwelcome, as evidently its appearance was the cause of the disappearance of our little visitors.

The writer took stories like these perfectly seriously, even though he knew that people might make fun of him for doing so. "What does it matter what anyone says of me," he once said to his mother in a letter. "I have a good hide by this time."

He did have a good hide. He had to, for he was famous all over England, and even in America and Australia. His name was Sir Arthur Conan Doyle.

Most people knew him as the creator of Sherlock Holmes, the world's most famous detective.

Sherlock Holmes was a keen-eyed, hawk-nosed man who had made detective work into a precise and rational science. Sherlock Holmes could put the tiniest clues together to find the truth. He was almost impossible to fool.

So it might seem surprising that his creator, Sir Arthur, believed in fairies. But he did.

To Sir Arthur, fairies were part of a spirit world that coexisted with the everyday world he saw all around him. The spirit world was invisible, though.

Only special people could see it or hear the voices of the spirits who lived in it. Those spirits included the ghosts of dead people, Sir Arthur believed. His own son, who had died of sickness after being wounded in the Great War, was one of them.

These days, Sir Arthur went to what were called séances, where he believed people called mediums might be able to give him messages from his son in the spirit world.

Sir Arthur had many friends who, like him, were interested in the invisible world. One day, Sir Arthur happened to be talking to a friend who asked him, had he heard the talk about some actual photographs of fairies? The friend hadn't actually seen them, but he had a friend who might know about it.

Sir Arthur talked to the friend, and then wrote a letter to a friend of that friend, and so on. He followed the trail of friends and relations until someone gave him Mr. Gardner's name.

When the two men met, Sir Arthur was relieved to see that Mr. Gardner seemed quite rational and respectable—not wild-eyed at all.

Sir Arthur and Mr. Gardner agreed that, together, they would conduct a step-by-step investigation of the matter of the fairy photographs.

Sir Arthur would handle the London end of the detective work.

Then the plan was that Mr. Gardner would take the train up to Cottingley, visit Elsie and her family, and see what kind of people they were.

If there was any sort of fraud involved, the two men thought, it would be best to uncover it right away.

Sir Arthur went to his men's club, the Athenaeum, and showed the fairy pictures to a friend of his, Sir Oliver Lodge, an expert in "psychic matters." Sir Oliver was skeptical: he suspected the ring of dancers had been somehow superimposed on a different background.

Sir Arthur didn't agree. "I argued that we had certainly traced the pictures to two children of the artisan [working] class, and that such photographic tricks would be entirely beyond them," he wrote.

Working-class children, surely, would not be able to pull off such a sophisticated trick.

Sir Arthur also took the two glass plates to Kingsway, a broad London boulevard where an American firm, the George Eastman Kodak Company, had built one of London's most modern buildings. There, Sir Arthur talked with two of Kodak's experts. "They examined the plates carefully, and neither of them could find any evidence of superposition, or other trick," Sir Arthur wrote.

The experts were not convinced the fairies were real—they thought that if a person had the right resources and knowledge, it was certainly possible to fake them.

Sir Arthur thought about this.

That meant that the only way to tell if the photographs were fake was to find out more about the girls who had taken them. Were they honest? Were they open?

What kind of girls *were* they?

TWELVE

Spider Girl

In Cottingley, at about that same time, Elsie picked up a paintbrush. In front of her on the white paper lay the penciled outlines of a mysterious young woman.

She wore a gown of spiderwebs. A spider dangled from her belt. A curious headdress, like a chambered seashell, framed the young woman's solemn face.

Elsie swirled her brush in color and began to paint.

Painting by Elsie, done the year she turned 19

She painted a golden band across the young woman's forehead. She painted golden snakes, with flickering tongues, curled at either end. She painted a green gargoyle sitting in the band, peering down.

She painted a tiny bat, its wings outstretched, hanging from the young woman's necklace.

Elsie finished the painting, and now a young woman stared back at her from the page, her green eyes narrowed.

The young woman had dark hair, like Elsie.

But Elsie's eyes were not green; they were a clear, bright blue. And all her life, Elsie had been deathly afraid of spiders.

What she was thinking when she painted that picture, no one would ever know.

For Elsie was a person with a secret she hadn't told her mother, or her father, or the man from London. And inside her, the secret was growing.

THIRTEEN

Sincerely Yours, Elsie Wright

The matter of actually going to see the girls had to be approached very carefully, Sir Arthur and Mr. Gardner agreed.

According to what Mr. Gardner had heard from various people, the girls were "very shy and reserved indeed," he informed Sir Arthur. "They are of a mechanic's family in Yorkshire, and the children are said to have played with fairies and elves in the woods near their village since babyhood."

The investigation couldn't be delayed too long, though. Mr. Gardner feared that, soon, the girls might not be able to see fairies anymore because they'd be too grown up. "Two children such as these are, are rare, and I fear now that we are late because almost certainly the inevitable will shortly happen, one of them will 'fall in love' and then—hey presto!!" Mr. Gardner wrote to Sir Arthur. Like something in a magician's trick, the girl's childhood would vanish.

Poof! And the chance to find out more about fairies would be gone.

So in June of 1920, Mr. Gardner wrote another letter to Elsie's mother. He mentioned that he'd had lantern slides made of the two photographs and was showing them to audiences in London. "Everyone who saw them was greatly interested. Indeed to say that many were excited about them would be understating the case," he wrote. Lots of people were asking for copies, he explained, and he thought it best to ask her (and perhaps she would also ask Miss Elsie, he added) about copyright issues. He offered to get

Elsie

the photos copyrighted himself, and he offered Miss
Elsie a percentage if she wanted it.

This time, Elsie wrote back herself.

31 Main St.
Cottingley Bingley
Yoks [Yorkshire]
June 14, 1920

Dear Mr. Gardner
   Please do just as you think best about the fairies, it is all
right to me, I'm glad the lantern slides have come out so well,
Mrs. Wright [a neighbor, not a relative, who happened to have the same last name] *told me how*
clear they had come out on the screen. Please excuse this bad
paper its the best I could get in the village
   Sincerely Yours
   Elsie Wright

She signed her name with a flourish.

❋   ❋   ❋

At the end of June, two more letters dropped through the mail slot at 31 Main Street. Both were from London, addressed to Miss Elsie Wright. One was from Mr. Gardner. The other, in neat, rounded handwriting, was on the stationery of a place called the Athenaeum.

June 30 [1920]

Dear Miss Elsie Wright

I have seen the wonderful pictures of the fairies which you and your cousin Frances have taken, and I have not been so interested for a long time. I will send you tomorrow one of my little books for I am sure you are not too old to enjoy adventures. I am going to Australia soon, but I only wish before I go that I could get to Bradford and have half an hours chat with you, for I should like to hear all about it. With best wishes

Yours sincerely

Arthur Conan Doyle

FOURTEEN

The Investigation

Elsie read the letter and the signature, and maybe she stared at it for a long moment.

For Sir Arthur Conan Doyle was one of her father's great heroes.

Sir Arthur Conan Doyle, according to her father, was more than just smart. Sir Arthur was Brilliant. Elsie's father had read all the Sherlock Holmes stories and Sir Arthur's other books, too, thrilling adventure tales, such as *The Lost World*.

Sir Arthur Conan Doyle was a very famous, very important, very high-class person.

When Elsie's father found out about the letter, he told her he was deeply worried. *Their family* was putting Important People's reputations on the line, he said. Her little joke had gone far enough! She should tell him what the trick was and be done with the whole silly business.

But Elsie didn't.

Elsie wouldn't.

Elsie never answered Sir Arthur's letter (or if she did, the letter has since been lost).

Instead, she wrote a letter to Mr. Gardner.

31 Main Street
Cottingley Bingley
July 1st [1920]

Dear Mr. Gardner
The photo of the fairies was taken instantaneous with

a very good light. I received a letter this morning from Sir
Arthur Conan Doyle witch was a great surprise. I had no idea
when I took the photo what a sensation it would cause.

> *I remain*
> *Yours Sincerely*
> *Elsie Wright*

(Flourish.)

After that, Elsie and her family went to the seaside
for a holiday, and when they got back, a package was
waiting. When Elsie unwrapped it, she found the
book Sir Arthur had promised to send. On a sky-
blue cover, gilt letters said: THE LOST WORLD.

The inside cover showed a flat-topped mountain
rising from a jungle. Waterfalls poured down from
a mysterious world, high above. The title page was
inscribed: *Yours sincerely, Arthur Conan Doyle, July 1920.*
Underneath, it said:

THE LOST WORLD
Being an account of the recent amazing

adventures of Professor George E. Challenger, Lord John Roxton, Professor Summerlee, and Mr. E. D. Malone of the "Daily Gazette."

A photograph captioned "The Members of the Exploring Party" showed four mustached and bearded men staring grimly at the camera. They did not look like the kind of people it was easy to fool. They looked like Important Men Who Got to the Bottom of Things.

But if Elsie felt a qualm, she didn't tell anybody.

Explorers aren't the only ones who can be brave. And besides, the Lost World was an interesting place. Anyone could see that just by paging through the illustrations.

One picture was "The Swamp of the Pterodactyls," another the "Glade of the Iguanodons." "The Central Lake" showed a sea monster's head and coils rising above the waves.

The book was two and a half inches thick and 319 pages long. A slow reader would require quite a bit of time to get through it. Still, it was nice of Sir Arthur to send it to her.

He had a vivid imagination—*that* much was clear.

Elsie's father, too, got a letter from Sir Arthur.

"I have seen the very interesting photos which your little girl took," it said. "They are certainly amazing. I was writing a little article for the *Strand* upon the evidence for the existence of fairies, so that I was very much interested. I should naturally like to use the photos, along with other material."

"I heard him moan to my Mother," Elsie wrote in a letter years later, " 'How could a brilliant man like him believe such a thing?' " How could *Sir Arthur Conan Doyle* be fooled?

And to think, her father said, that the great man had been bamboozled by "our Elsie, and she at the bottom of her class."

Elsie's father wrote Sir Arthur back.

❉   ❉   ❉

"The Members of the Exploring Party." Photograph from Elsie's copy of *The Lost World*.

31 Main Street
Cottingley, Bingley
July 12, 1920

Dear Sir,

I hope you will forgive us for not answering your letter sooner and thanking you for the beautiful book you so kindly sent to Elsie. She is delighted with it. I can assure you we do appreciate the honour you have done her. The book came last Saturday morning an hour after we had left for the seaside for our holidays, so we did not receive it until last night. We received a letter from Mr. Gardner at the same time, and he proposes coming to see us at the end of July. Would it be too long to wait until then, when we could explain what we know about it?

Yours very gratefully,
Arthur Wright

In his letter, Sir Arthur had asked if he or Mr. Gardner might run up to Cottingley and have a little chat with the girls. Elsie's father's reply—"*Mr. Gardner . . . proposes coming to see us at the end of July. Would it be too long to wait until then?"*—very politely hinted that it would be best if Sir Arthur didn't come.

So Elsie's father never met his hero.

But one afternoon in late July, Elsie's mother opened their front door to a quiet middle-aged man in a brown suit and a bow tie.

Elsie's mother showed Mr. Gardner into the parlor and introduced Elsie. (Mr. Gardner remembered her later as "a shy, pretty girl of about sixteen.") The three of them made conversation until Elsie's father came home from work and they all had tea.

Mr. Gardner asked Elsie's father to tell his part of the story. Elsie's father said he'd put just one plate in the camera, given it to Elsie and Frances, and then developed the pictures as soon as they came back.

Elsie's mother told Mr. Gardner she remembered quite well that the two girls were gone from the house only a short time.

Mr. Gardner examined Elsie's hand—some critics of the gnome picture had said Elsie's hand looked suspiciously large. "She laughingly made me promise not to say much about it, it is so very long!" he wrote later. Mr. Gardner traced the outline of Elsie's hand on a piece of paper, for evidence.

And then, after tea, Elsie and Mr. Gardner went down to the beck. "I was glad of the opportunity of questioning the elder girl quietly by herself and of talking things over," Mr. Gardner wrote later.

Mr. Gardner looked at the waterfall and the nearby toadstools. He took his own photographs of the exact spots where the fairy photos were taken. He asked Elsie what color the fairies were.

Elsie told him they were "the palest of green, pink, mauve," he wrote later. "Much more in the wings than in the bodies, which are very pale to white." The gnome, she told him, seemed to be wearing black tights, a reddish-brown jersey, and a red pointed cap.

Elsie explained that she couldn't entice them in, since she had no power of her own over the fairies. The way to get them to come close, she said, was to just sit quietly and think about fairies. Then, when you heard a faint rustling or saw something moving in the distance, you just waved to them, to show them they were welcome.

Mr. Gardner asked Elsie about the gnome's wings. Both he and Sir Arthur thought that the markings seemed to look like those on a moth's wing.

Elsie explained that they weren't wing markings but musical pipes. She added that on days when there wasn't too much rustling in the wood, you could hear the faint, high sound of gnome music.

Mr. Gardner's visit lasted two days. Before he left, Elsie told him she'd very much like to send him a picture of a fairy flying. There seemed little chance of that happening, though, since Elsie said she couldn't take pictures of fairies unless Frances was with her. And of course, Frances was far away in Scarborough.

Mr. Gardner said perhaps Frances could come and spend her summer holidays in Cottingley? Then the two girls could take pictures of fairies together? He could just run up to Scarborough and see Frances's parents about it.

And what could Elsie say then? She'd already gone

and told Mr. Gardner she wanted to take a picture of a fairy flying!

The grown-ups seemed to think Frances would be *happy* to visit. And *of course* she'd want to take pictures of fairies. . . .

PART THREE

Frances and Elsie

FIFTEEN

Frances Comes for a Visit

Nobody asked Frances, of course. The next thing *she* knew, it had all been worked out.

There was Mr. Gardner, sitting at the dinner table: a boring man in brown with nothing at all interesting to say. And now, because of him, she had to go to Cottingley and take pictures of fairies. The grown-ups had it all worked out.

Frances couldn't call Elsie on the telephone and ask her what to do: neither of them *had* a telephone.

She couldn't write. What if somebody found the letter?

August came, and in Scarborough the ocean was as warm as it would get all year. Frances's friends were no doubt out swimming and running barefoot on the sand. And Frances? Frances was on her way to Cottingley, watching the Yorkshire countryside roll past.

Green hills. Stone fences. Sheep.

When Frances finally got to Cottingley, Aunt Polly did not seem to be her usual cheerful self, at least when it came to fairies.

"If Elsie takes one flying as she said she would, I will be quite satisfied about them," she had written to Mr. Gardner. "And yet to doubt is worse, for then I must think they are not trouthfull, not a very happy state of mind to be in, is it, and yet I have never found either Elsie or Frances tell a lie. Please don't blame me for feeling like that, it's because the whole thing is so strange."

Frances didn't need to see the letter to tell that something had changed. She felt "horribly uncomfortable," she wrote later. "It wasn't a joke anymore. People were taking it too seriously and it had all got out of hand."

Aunt Polly was even keeping Elsie home from work so the girls could go out to the beck together and take plenty of pictures.

After all, Mr. Gardner had sent Elsie an expensive new camera and *six dozen* glass plates.

When they were alone, Elsie told Frances she had painted two fairies, one for herself and one for Frances. She said they'd take two pictures and be done with it. The fairies were both cut out and ready.

Elsie's fairy wore an evening dress and a fashionable bob haircut. In one hand, she held a bouquet of bell-shaped blue flowers. Harebells, they were called.

Frances's fairy wasn't wearing much of anything but some tights and wisp of gauze. Elsie had drawn

Elsie and the harebell fairy

her leaping into the air, her arms outstretched and her toes pointed. Frances didn't think Elsie had gotten the back leg right, but it would have to do.

That night, Elsie and Frances wound their wet hair over rags and then slept on them, with the lumps digging into their heads. When they untied their hair the next morning, it was curled in long ringlets.

The day was gray and misty, not (they had told the grown-ups) the kind of weather that was good for taking pictures of fairies. But by afternoon it cleared.

Aunt Polly went to have tea with Aunt Clara so that Frances and Elsie could be alone. "I . . . left them to it," she later wrote Mr. Gardner.

Elsie and Frances put on dresses trimmed with lace and ruffles, tied a big white bow in Frances's hair, and went down the path to the beck.

They stuck Elsie's painted fairy to a branch. Elsie put her head down near, so it looked as though the fairy were offering her the bouquet.

Frances measured the distance the camera should

be from Elsie. The two girls agreed on a shutter speed, Frances pushed the shutter, and "the deed was done," Frances wrote later.

Next, they went to Frances's willow tree. They stuck Frances's leaping fairy onto one of its branches. The light was dim, which meant they would have to set the shutter to stay open for a long time. Frances stood so her face was in profile with the fairy's little knee just a few inches from her nose. She looked at the slip of paper in a friendly sort of way and kept her head quite still, so the image would not be blurred.

Elsie pulled the lever, and that was that.

"We wandered home, taking our time," Frances wrote later. "We saw the baby frogs were no longer babies, the blackberries were still green but after the rain were beginning to fatten. I had no feeling of regret that I would not be there to pick and eat them, nor even that after this week my little men would be in my past."

Uncle Arthur took the camera and disappeared into his darkroom. When he emerged with the

Frances and the leaping fairy

photographs, Aunt Polly was disappointed to see that there were only two.

After that, it rained, and Elsie and Frances said they couldn't take fairy pictures in the rain.

Aunt Polly told them they were very ungrateful. She'd written to Mr. Gardner telling him how excited Elsie was to have the camera and what a handsome present it was, and now all they had to show for *six dozen* plates were two pictures?

It would not do.

But day after day, it kept raining.

On the afternoon of the last day of Frances's visit, Aunt Polly sent them out of the house, rain or no rain. Then she and Uncle Arthur went out with some friends for a drive in the countryside and locked the door behind them. They would be gone all afternoon.

"The weather was gloomy and we were gloomy," Frances remembered later. "It was a hopeless task."

In their raincoats, Frances and Elsie wandered down the garden path and into the beck. Frances caught a glimpse of little men, but they were off in the distance.

After a while, she and Elsie climbed up the banks to the high ground around the beck, the place where once (very long ago now) Elsie had taken the gnome picture. They wandered toward a little grove of trees and sat down.

They both agreed that if anyone wanted them to take more photos next year, they would say no.

Not far from them lay a little tangle of grass and leaves with drops of rainwater clinging to it. It didn't look like much more than an old bird's nest.

Afterward, they couldn't agree which one of them took a picture of it, but neither of them thought it looked like much at the time. It was probably just a waste of a plate.

Then they wandered on home.

By the time Aunt Polly and Uncle Arthur returned, it was too late to develop the plate—Uncle Arthur needed daylight, shining through the darkroom's red windowpane. It wasn't until the next day that Aunt

Polly found out that the girls had taken only one picture.

"It's a queer one, we can't make it out," she wrote to Mr. Gardner.

In a letter Elsie wrote years later, she said that all that she and Frances could see when they looked at the photograph were "faded-out bits showing of wings and faces here and there . . . bits of dead leaves (that could have been wings) or shadows (that might have been faces)."

Aunt Polly didn't tell Mr. Gardner that she was sorry and disappointed to have so few pictures to show for all the plates he'd sent. She just wrote, at the end of her letter, "She didn't take one flying after all."

SIXTEEN

An Epoch-Making Event

Frances went home to Scarborough. Summer ended and school began.

Elsie had another job now, in a Christmas-card factory in the hills above Bradford. All day long, she sprayed brown paint on reindeer, red paint on Father Christmas, and so on, for card after card after card.

The days grew shorter and colder. Dark fell early. Outside the factory, the real world began to look more like Christmas.

Then one day, in late November, Elsie received a hastily written letter from Mr. Gardner. "I send just this line at once as the *Strand* is out today and I am already getting numerous inquiries about the fairies," Mr. Gardner wrote.

Elsie couldn't just run out and buy one in the village, since there weren't any shops that sold magazines in Cottingley. But when she did find a copy of the *Strand*, there was the headline, right on the front cover.

FAIRIES PHOTOGRAPHED

AN EPOCH-MAKING EVENT DESCRIBED BY

A. CONAN DOYLE

Inside were the photos of Elsie and the gnome and Frances and the dancing fairies. They were "the two most astounding photographs ever published," the article said.

"Should the incidents here narrated, and the photographs attached, hold their own against the criticism which they will excite, it is no exaggeration to say that they will mark an epoch in human thought," Sir Arthur wrote. "I put them and all the evidence

Cover of *The Strand Magazine*, December 1920

before the public for examination and judgment." Sir Arthur added that there was no "final and absolute proof" that the photographs were genuine. But he himself considered the case to be very strong.

Sir Arthur admitted that at one point, he and Mr. Gardner had suspected that Elsie might have painted the fairies. "Mr. Gardner, however, tested her powers of drawing, and found that, while she could do landscapes cleverly, the fairy figures which she had attempted in imitation of those she had seen were entirely uninspired, and bore no possible resemblance to those in the photograph."

Entirely uninspired.

Elsie remembered those words for the rest of her life.

"They threw cold water over the one thing I thought I was good at," she wrote many years later, "my drawing and paintings that hung in our house."

Elsie couldn't say *she* drew the fairies in the photographs, for that would have given everything away. She could only keep reading as Sir Arthur raved about the beauty of the little dancing figures. "There is an ornamental rim to the pipe of the elves which shows that the graces of art are not unknown among them. And what joy is in the complete abandon of their little graceful figures as they let themselves go in the dance!" he wrote.

But *Elsie,* of course, could not have drawn them. Oh, indeed not.

For Elsie was a country girl. Elsie was an artisan's child.

And Elsie was not a good enough artist.

Sir Arthur hadn't wanted tour buses packed with people coming to Cottingley to see the fairies, so he had made up a false name for the village. He gave Frances and Elsie fake names, too: Alice and Iris Carpenter.

Alice and Iris Carpenter, the mysterious fairy girls . . .

In a portrait taken that summer in Cottingley, Frances/Alice is standing in the back garden of 31 Main Street in front of a big clump of daisies. She's smiling shyly, wearing her white lace dress and big hair ribbon. She does not look at all mysterious.

But, in her portrait, also taken that summer, Elsie/ Iris leans against a tree in the woods, near the spot where the gnome picture was taken. She's dressed in something an artist or a person in a play might wear: a peaked fur cap and a dark, folktale kind of dress. She stands at a distance from the camera, so it's hard to see her expression. Her long hands are hidden in her pockets.

Reporters soon figured out who Iris and Alice Carpenter really were and where they lived.

In Scarborough, Frances hated it when the newspapermen tried to interview her.

To avoid them, she snuck to school by cutting through a back lane toward the sea, then taking a roundabout way through the streets. After school, she would walk in a crowd of other girls and hide her face by pulling her scarf up and letting her braids swing forward. When reporters did find her, she'd tell them it was nice up the beck, and yes, she did see fairies.

And after that, they didn't seem much interested in what she had to say.

Elsie was working in the upper room at the Christmas-card factory when a message came from the front office: a reporter was asking to see her. He was from a London newspaper, the *Westminster Gazette.*

Elsie sent a message back saying she didn't want to be interviewed. But the reporter sent another message, asking again.

So Elsie went down to the front office and stood behind the low counter. She was tall and slender and very pretty. Her thick auburn hair was tied back with a narrow gold band that went all around her head.

She told the reporter she was "fed up" with the fairies and didn't want to talk, but he began to question her anyway.

He asked her where the fairies came from, and she said she didn't know.

Did she see them coming?

"Yes."

Then, the reporter said, she must have seen where they came from.

Elsie hesitated, then laughed and said she couldn't say.

Where did they go after dancing near her?

Elsie said she couldn't say.

After that, Elsie didn't want to answer any more questions, but the reporter wouldn't leave. Perhaps, he suggested, the fairies "simply vanished into the air."

"Yes," said Elsie.

Elsie told him the fairies didn't speak to her, and she didn't speak to them. She and Frances were the only ones who saw them. "If anybody else were there," she said, "the fairies would not come out."

The reporter seemed puzzled. He asked her to explain further, but all she would do was smile and say, "You don't understand."

Elsie told him that these days, it was getting harder to see fairies. The fairies' shapes were more "transparent" now. Before, they were "rather hard."

"You see," Elsie explained, "we were young then."

The reporter didn't seem to understand, but Elsie wouldn't add anything more.

When the article came out in the newspaper, the headline said:

DO FAIRIES EXIST?

INVESTIGATION IN A YORKSHIRE VALLEY

COTTINGLEY'S MYSTERY

STORY OF THE GIRL WHO TOOK THE SNAPSHOT

"My mission to Yorkshire was to secure evidence, if possible, which would prove or disprove the claim that fairies existed. I frankly confess that I failed," the reporter wrote.

Elsie the school-leaver, Elsie the best-of-the-worst-or-the-worst-of-the-best, had outwitted the man from the London newspaper.

After that, reporters thought Elsie might have used trick photography to fake the fairies. So they went to Gunston's Photography Studio and asked Mr. Gunston about her.

Mr. Gunston didn't even know who she was. After a while, he got mad that reporters kept coming around and asking about some little nobody who used to work in his basement.

When Elsie found out, she wished she could have seen Mr. Gunston's face.

~

SEVENTEEN

The Fairy Bower

The newspapers didn't come right out and call Elsie a liar, but they came close.

"I would suggest to Miss Elsie that she has carried her little joke quite far enough, and that she should tell the public what the 'fairies' really are," proclaimed the *Times* of London.

"I know children," someone wrote in a London magazine. "And knowing children, and knowing that Sir Arthur Conan Doyle has legs, I decide that the Miss Carpenters have pulled one of them."

It never seemed to occur to the newspaper writers that if Elsie and Frances said it was all a joke now, their parents wouldn't think it was one bit funny— and Elsie and Frances would be in deep, deep trouble.

Mr. Gardner was sorry, he wrote to Elsie's mother, that the reporters had been coming around and pestering, but "with your help in Cottingley we will bring everything through quite all right yet. And none of you shall have the least cause to regret letting the photographs become public if I can help it. We will win through and Elsie and Frances shall be justified everywhere."

Elsie's mother wrote back, of course, as she always did. Her letters to Mr. Gardner were longer now, and friendlier. Elsie's mother believed in the fairies now, just the way Mr. Gardner did. For surely, her daughter would never lie to her!

She believed Mr. Gardner when he said that soon the truth would come out, and that after that, no one would say Elsie and Frances were lying, ever again.

Mr. Gardner wrote to Elsie's father, too, informing him that he, Mr. Gardner, had a secret weapon in the fight: the latest fairy photos. "I am keeping them back for the present because I want to keep them in reserve to sweep the board at the proper moment!" he wrote.

Elsie's father wasn't happy at all. And no matter how many times he asked Elsie what the trick was, she wouldn't tell him.

Mr. Gardner wrote both Elsie and Frances, telling them to lock any copies of the newest fairy photos away in a secret place and tell no one outside the family.

But why would Elsie and Frances want anyone to know there were *more* fairy photographs? Things were bad enough with just the first two!

And besides, they had only taken the blue-flower

fairy and the leaping fairy photos because the grown-ups made them.

And as for the last one . . . it was only shadows and tangles of grass. Why should they tell anybody about *that*?

Winter began to fade. Spring approached.

In bookstores and shop windows across England, the *Strand*'s Christmas issue had been replaced by the January issue, and then the February issue.

Then came the March issue.

"The Evidence for Fairies by A. Conan Doyle With New Fairy Photographs" said the headline on the front cover.

Inside were the pictures of the leaping fairy and the flower-bearing fairy. But the most exciting photograph of all, according to Mr. Gardner, was the third one. Mr. Gardner called it the "fairy's bower."

In the photograph, one fairy, her wings showing clearly, was "apparently considering whether it is time to get up. An early riser of more mature age is seen on the right possessing abundant hair and wonderful wings," Mr. Gardner had written to Sir Arthur.

"We have now succeeded in bringing this print out splendidly," Mr. Gardner wrote. "Never before, or otherwhere, surely, has a fairy's bower been photographed!"

He didn't say exactly what he meant by "bringing out" the print.

But now, there were fairy outlines in it that neither Elsie nor Frances had noticed before.

One afternoon, just as school ended, Frances and the other girls in her class were packing up their satchels to go home when the Headmaster came into the classroom.

He called Frances up to the teacher's desk, and there, in front of all the other girls, he began to ask her questions about fairies.

"Well," he said after a few minutes, "it would be interesting to have a few here in the classrooms." Then he walked out.

The other girls all stared at her, and Frances felt like a "perfect fool." Afterward, the other girls teased her about it. "Thinking about fairies, then?" they'd say if Frances didn't answer a question right away.

"This is what I hated for years," she wrote in her autobiography, "when people looked at me as though I weren't normal and treated me as someone different from any other schoolgirl. . . . I was a normal ordinary girl and no one was going to look big-eyed at me or ask questions I didn't want to answer."

Frances promised herself she would never take another photograph.

Ever.

Mr. Gardner didn't think Frances was a normal, ordinary girl at all.

He believed she had the power to see things that were invisible to most people.

He'd thought so from the very first time he met her—Frances was "mediumistic." There was something about her that seemed to float outside her body, he noticed. He believed that airy, floating substance, which he called "subtle ectoplasmic or etheric material," was what attracted nature spirits to her. It also made the nature spirits themselves solidify a bit, so that a camera could take their picture.

And yet . . . Frances didn't seem to want to take photographs at all—even when he'd sent her her own camera in Scarborough and her own six dozen plates. All he'd gotten back was a polite note.

Still, Frances wasn't the only one in the world who could see things that other people couldn't.

Mr. Gardner had a friend named Mr. Hodson, who was quite well known as a "clairvoyant," or seer of hidden things. Why not bring *him* to the fairy glen?

Mr. Hodson might be able to take some photographs, and not just ordinary still photos. Perhaps Mr. Hodson could even take some *moving* pictures, with a cinema camera!

So Mr. Gardner invited the clairvoyant (and his wife) to come spend a few days in Cottingley.

Mr. Gardner picked the last week of Frances's summer holidays. That way, Frances and Elsie and

Mr. and Mrs. Hodson could all go out to the beck together to look for fairies.

You probably know how Frances felt when she found out.

This time, she had to miss *Cricket Week,* when all the cricket stars came to Scarborough.

She and Elsie would have to tromp through the beck with a bunch of strangers. And as if that weren't bad enough, they'd have to sit there, hour after hour, waiting for fairies.

Frances decided that even if she did see any, she wouldn't say a word. If Mr. Hodson wanted fairies, fine. He could just see one for himself.

EIGHTEEN

The Glen Was Swarming

Frances, Elsie, Mr. Hodson, and Mrs. Hodson sat in the woods, next to the basket of sandwiches they'd packed for lunch. It was August, but they all wore coats, for it had been drizzling rain when they set off that morning.

Mr. Hodson had brought a still camera, a cinema camera, and a field notebook. Mrs. Hodson took out her knitting.

Mr. Hodson turned out to be the kind of person who is forever bringing up the names of important people he just happens to know. His wife was older than he was, and he was always turning to her and saying things like "Happy, darling?" then giving her a little smile.

The sun moved slowly through the gray, dull sky. Mrs. Hodson's knitting needles clicked.

After a while, Mr. Hodson began to speak in half whispers about his Experiences in the Occult World.

Frances listened carefully to the pompous, flowery way he talked so that she'd be able to imitate it later to amuse her friends. But after a while even that was boring.

Finally, after what seemed like hours and hours and *hours,* Elsie said she saw a fairy.

"Yes, yes," said Mr. Hodson eagerly. He added that the fairy was materializing.

Elsie said she saw one nearly six feet tall, standing by a tree.

Mr. Hodson said he saw it, too — it was chained to the tree. It was the spirit of the tree. . . .

He began scribbling in his notebook.

And then—they couldn't seem to help it—both Elsie and Frances started pretending they saw fairies. "Our normal selves came to the surface," Frances admitted later.

And it *was* funny, though they didn't dare laugh.

Mr. Hodson wrote:

GNOMES AND FAIRIES. *In the field we saw figures about the size of the gnome. They were making weird faces and grotesque contortions at the group. One in particular took great delight in knocking his knees together. These forms appeared to Elsie singly—one dissolving and another appearing in its place. I, however, saw them in a group with one figure more prominently visible than the rest. Elsie saw also a gnome like the one in the photograph, but not so bright and not coloured. . . .*

WATER NYMPH. *In the beck itself, near the large rock, at a slight fall in the water, I saw a water sprite. It was an entirely nude female figure with long fair hair, which it appeared to be combing or passing through its fingers. . . . Its form was of a dazzling rosy whiteness, and its face very beautiful. . . . It showed no consciousness of my presence, and, though I waited with the camera in the hope of taking it, it did not detach itself from the surroundings in which it was in some way merged. . . .*

WOOD ELVES. (*Under the old beeches in the wood, Cottingley, August 12, 1921.*) *Two tiny wood elves came racing over the ground past us as we sat on a fallen tree trunk. Seeing us, they pulled up short about five feet away, and stood regarding us with considerable amusement but no fear. . . . As Frances came up and sat within a foot of them they withdrew, as if in alarm, a distance of eight feet or so, where they remained apparently regarding us and comparing notes of their impressions. . . .*

WATER FAIRY. (*August 14, 1921.*) *This creature hung poised . . . much as a seagull supports itself against the wind. . . . I did not notice any wings.*

FAIRY, ELVES, GNOMES, AND BROWNIE. (*Sunday, August 14, 9 p.m. In the field.*) *Lovely still moonlit evening. The field appears to be densely populated with native spirits of various kinds. . . . Frances sees tiny fairies dancing in a circle, the figures gradually expanding in size till they reached eighteen inches, the ring widening in proportion. Elsie sees a vertical circle of dancing fairies*

flying slowly round. . . . (Written by the light of the moon.) I see
couples a foot high . . . dancing in a slow waltz-like motion in the
middle of the field. . . . Elsie sees a small imp.

On the afternoon of Thursday, August 18, Mr.
Hodson was overcome by an especially beautiful
creature who moved her arms, fluttered her butter-
fly wings, and then smiled at him, placing her finger
on her lips. Her body appeared to be clothed only in
"iridescent shimmering golden light."

Honestly.

What could Elsie and Frances say to *that* one?

Elsie made a pencil sketch that showed Elsie and
Frances dancing together to a ragtime tune. "When
we two one step," she wrote underneath.

It was a funny sketch, quick and laughing, like
Elsie herself. Frances in the picture is mock serious,
clowning around. They looked, dancing together, as
though they shared a joke that only the two of them
understood.

One day when they went out in the fields with Mr. Hodson, Elsie took a photograph of his plump, tweed-clad bottom as he crouched in the long grass, waiting for fairies.

A few times that August, Elsie and Frances's little cousin Marjorie came along. After a while she said she saw fairies, too. Elsie took a picture of her dancing in the woods. Later, Elsie colored it in, so that Marjorie almost looked like a fairy herself.

Still, it was a long week.

In one photograph taken then, Elsie, Frances, and Mr. Hodson stand uneasily in front of a window, its dark surface reflecting shadows and sky.

Frances wears a cautious smile. Elsie's expression is guarded, her eyes slightly narrowed, her head turned to the side.

She looks like a person who is getting very, very tired of fairies.

Mr. Gardner came to visit for part of the week and gazed unhappily into the camera as he had his picture

Mr. Hodson looking for fairies. Photo by Elsie.

Cousin Marjorie in the woods

taken with Elsie, Frances, and Mrs. Hodson. In the photograph, Elsie and Frances are each wearing their cameras. Yet they have not taken a single photo of a fairy.

Mr. Hodson, too, has for some reason failed to take any, with either the still camera or the cinema camera.

When Sir Arthur heard what had happened, it seemed to him that the "change in the girls" was the main reason why they couldn't take any more pictures of fairies. It was too late now. Like the rabbit in a magician's trick, *Hey, presto!* The girls' simplicity and innocence had vanished. It was just as Mr. Gardner had feared, in the letter he had sent to Sir Arthur long ago.

Now when the fairies came near Frances and Elsie, the bright, airy substance of which fairies were made no longer became solid. It wouldn't show up on a photograph.

It was a pity, really, but that was the way fairies were.

NINETEEN

A Gentle See-through Fade-out

Elsie said it, too: the fairies were gone.

"When the last fairy pictures were taken . . . they were doing a gentle see-through fade-out on us, especially that last mixed-up one. . . . ," she once wrote in a letter. "No more fairies appeared so it was just a waste snapping away at nothing, for definitely that was the end of it all."

Neither Elsie nor Frances ever took another fairy photograph.

❋   ❋   ❋

Six years later, Mr. Gardner stood on the deck of an ocean liner bound for America. In his luggage were lantern slides of the five Cottingley Fairy Photographs, as they were now known.

"Briton in U.S. to Prove Fairies Exist," a New York newspaper announced. "Champion of Elfs Struts His Stuff," read the mocking headline in another. "A Bit of Britain's Gnome-land," commented the caption above the photograph of Elsie and the flower-bearing fairy—as though anyone could see how ridiculous it all was.

In California, the *Los Angeles Examiner* ran the photograph of Frances and the fairy ring with a caption that simpered, "Really, Truly They're Fairies."

Still, Mr. Gardner toured all over America. Everywhere he went, he showed slides of Elsie and Frances and the fairies.

He knew what he believed in.

Sir Arthur wrote a book about Elsie and Frances's pictures. He called it *The Coming of the Fairies.*

Science, Sir Arthur now believed, was like a harsh

light that left the world hard and bare, "like a landscape in the moon." And surely, there was more to life than that! Just knowing that fairies were out there, even if you never got to see one, added charm and romance to the world.

Sir Arthur didn't say this in his book, but a part of him had longed for fairies ever since he was a boy. His uncle Richard painted wonderful pictures of fairies: little creatures who lived in a world of soft sunlight and bright flowers. They hid under leaves, and you could see them if you just knew where to look.

Sir Arthur's father drew fairies, too. One of his watercolors showed a fairy band streaming down from a starlit sky to alight in the grim, gray courtyard of an insane asylum.

Sir Arthur's father lived in that insane asylum. He'd gone away, never to return, when Sir Arthur was seventeen. In the asylum, Sir Arthur's father drew pictures of tiny people holding leaves as big as umbrellas or lurking in flowerpots or riding on the backs of birds.

Sir Arthur didn't mention any of that in *The Coming*

of the Fairies. But if fairies were *real,* Sir Arthur's father wasn't crazy after all.

If fairies were *real,* the world was a happier place.

As he drew toward the end of his life, Sir Arthur had statues of gnomes set out in his garden, hoping that fairies would be drawn to them. He even had his gardener's little girl sit next to the statues to increase the chances.

For fairies seemed to like little girls.

Elsie and Frances grew up and got married. And still, they kept their secret.

Elsie immigrated to America, where no one knew who she was. There she met a man named Frank Hill, who liked to laugh as much as she did. Elsie and Frank got married and sailed away on an ocean liner for India, where they lived for many years.

Elsie got to see the snow-covered peaks of Darjeeling. She sent home postcards of the pyramids and of the minarets and bazaars of Cairo. She saw monkeys and palm trees. She rode horses and explored jungles and swam in the ocean. She saw a white stone temple rising out of a jungle on an island in Malaysia, like the mysterious cliffs rising out of the jungle in *The Lost World*.

Elsie never told her husband the secret of the cutouts, but it didn't seem to matter. "My husband always says he believes in fairies," she once wrote, "but he always says it in the middle of when he is laughing."

Back in England, no one knew who Frances was. She could daydream all she wanted now and nobody asked her if she was thinking about fairies.

She danced the Charleston, just like any carefree, pretty young woman. She went on vacation and sent back a picture of herself in a grass skirt, signed "Love, Frances."

In a long white gown and pearls, Frances married a soldier named Cecil Wilfred Way. She felt it was only right to tell him about the fairies, so she did. "It was one of those things that I thought he'd better know," she told someone once. "And he believed me—always believed me."

Frances in a grass skirt

For years and years, Frances never saw another fairy. Then another war started: the Second World War. Frances began to worry, just as she'd worried when she was only nine and her father went away to what was now called the First World War.

Frances's husband worked long hours, preparing for the great invasion of Europe that would decide whether England and its allies won the war or lost to Nazi Germany. Frances's husband got sick and lost weight, and Frances got so worried that she had horrible headaches.

Then one day, Frances was standing in the kitchen with a headache when she looked down and saw a fairy man gazing up at her.

She ran from the room.

After that, she began to wonder if being worried and seeing fairies had anything to do with each other.

Sometimes, too, it seemed to Frances that she could hear people's thoughts. It was very unpleasant, hearing what people were thinking as if they had spoken out loud, and Frances was glad when it went away.

These days when she thought about the fairies,

The fairy's bower

it seemed as though they'd haunted her all her life. She got a creepy feeling when she looked at the picture of herself with the dancing fairies. Their wings were much too large for real fairy wings. And the little gnome had a sinister look on his face.

But the last photo, the one that Mr. Gardner had called the fairy's bower, was different. She knew now that Mr. Gardner had been right about the last photo.

There *were* fairies, real ones, in among the grasses.

TWENTY

Fairy Grandmothers

Frances had two children, a boy named David and a girl named Christine.

One day when the grown-ups were gone, David and Christine had nothing much to do. So together, they went exploring in the house.

They snuck into their mother's bedroom and rummaged around in her cupboard. On the second shelf, they found a book wrapped in brown paper. They leafed through the pages—and there, sitting in front of a waterfall and gazing straight at them, was their mother as a little girl. A ring of fairies seemed to be dancing all around her.

The book was called *The Coming of the Fairies.*

David and Christine put the book back in the cupboard, exactly where they'd found it. They closed the door and never said a word to anybody.

Years went by, and one day when David was seventeen and Christine was fifteen, they happened to be talking about a science-fiction story they'd both read. It was about hidden worlds that existed right alongside the everyday world and how, if conditions were right, the two worlds could meet. David and Christine were deep in conversation when they realized that their mother was there in the room.

In a quiet voice, she told Christine to go to the cupboard in the bedroom and bring back a book, covered in brown paper, that she would find on the second shelf. Christine handed it to her in silence. Then their mother told them about the fairies.

David didn't think they were real, but Christine was thrilled.

Her own mother had seen fairies!

"Now I've told you," her mother said, "and I never want to hear about it again."

Elsie was looking through a magazine once when she saw a cruel cartoon of Sir Arthur. It showed him squinting dreamily into the sky with Sherlock Holmes chained to his ankles and a cloud of smoke around his head.

But Sir Arthur would never know he'd been deceived.

Mr. Gardner would never be heartbroken.

Elsie's mother and father would never find out that their daughter had lied.

Because as long as they lived, Elsie would never, ever tell.

Elsie had one child, a boy named Glenn.

Glenn grew up in India with his mother and father and their pet parrot. Outside their windows lay a green courtyard where banana trees grew.

Glenn's granny Polly lived with them, too. She

had come to India after her husband, Glenn's grandfather, whom he had never met, died back in England. She was a cheerful, funny old lady. Glenn loved her dearly, almost as though she were his own mother.

In the long, still afternoons, with the ceiling fans stirring the hot air, she used to tell him stories about life back home in England.

And one day, when Glenn was ten, his granny told him about the fairies.

He could tell from the way she talked that his granny believed in fairies, but he didn't, not for a minute.

His granny thought the fairies were a thrilling secret. But when Glenn's mother found out he'd been told, she got so angry that it made Glenn's granny cry, and he had to put his arms around her to comfort her.

Glenn's mother told him never to tell anyone, ever. Reporters would come around! It would be as bad as it was in England!

She didn't have to worry, though. Why should he

tell anyone? Why would he want people laughing at him about a bunch of stupid fairies?

Years and years later, when someone asked him if he was named after the fairy glen, he said of course not. *Glen* has only one *n*. His name had two.

And fairies were absolute nonsense.

Glenn and David and Christine grew up and had children of their own. So now Elsie and Frances were grandmothers.

Frances's daughter, Christine, still believed in fairies. "She's never been skeptical—she's always been thrilled to bits. And she's talked about it to my grandchildren all the time," Frances once told someone.

Frances couldn't tell her daughter and her grandchildren that she and Elsie had lied.

So they kept the secret, still.

One day, Frances was looking out the window when she saw a van pulling up. The letters on its side said BBC, which stood for *British Broadcasting Corporation*.

She knew right away what they'd come for.

Elsie had moved back to England from India, and somehow, a reporter had learned who she was. Now they were after Frances.

Frances hated it, just as she always had. But Elsie . . . Elsie rather liked it when reporters came around.

She still had "a touch of 1920s dash about her," one journalist who met Elsie when she was an old lady wrote. "She has a dazzling smile and a laugh that—if laughs are really infectious—could lay low half of the county."

Elsie stood tall—five feet ten inches—and was still slender. She still kept a parrot for a pet, and she still loved a good costume. She'd wear a big hat with a feather in it and gloves even when she was just waiting for the bus. Every morning, she put on rouge and bright-red lipstick.

When television reporters interviewed her, she'd watch herself on television later—she once joked that she wanted to see if she looked any better in color than she did in black and white.

In time, a Yorkshire television station invited her to come back to Cottingley to be interviewed there. On the day of the interview, she wore a red turtleneck, and a coat with a leopard-skin collar. She set her black hat at a jaunty angle, tilted above one eye.

Frances was invited to Yorkshire, too. It had been years since she'd been to Cottingley, so she said she'd go. She wore a raincoat and sensible shoes.

When they got to Cottingley, they rode in a television van with a man named Joe Cooper. "Mind if I turn this on?" he asked them, motioning to his tape recorder. "I'm very interested in collecting data."

"They say, jointly, calmly and lightly, that they don't mind at all," he wrote in a book, *The Case of the Cottingley Fairies.* "They chat amiably and naturally together as the tape circles. . . . When they laugh, which is often, there is a high, spontaneous tinkling about it all, and my fancy thinks there *is* something when the pair of them get together."

"Once I was talking to this doctor's wife," Elsie told him. "She said, 'Come on, Elsie, tell us how you did it—I mean, well, it must have been trickery because . . . well . . . *you* don't believe in fairies, do you, Elsie?' " And at that, both Elsie and Frances gave high peals of laughter.

They had "an air of mystery and gentleness and holding back something," Joe Cooper noticed.

This time when Elsie and Frances went down the garden path to the beck, a television reporter and a cameraman came, too. A soundman wearing headphones and wielding a huge microphone on a beam scurried along beside them.

At the spot where the waterfall was, the whole group came to a halt. The reporter had Frances sit by the waterfall, put her chin on her hand, and gaze at the camera.

When they came to the field where the huge oaks grew, Elsie had to sit down and hold out her hand the exact same way she'd done in the gnome photograph.

The whole time, the reporter asked questions.

Elsie and Frances answered with open, smiling

faces. They looked at each other and laughed, especially when he asked them about Mr. Hodson. Mr. Hodson was a phony, they said. He was preposterous! He'd even written a book. . . .

"How big were the fairies?" the reporter asked.

Elsie and Frances glanced at each other. After a tiny pause, Frances held her hand low to the ground. "This big."

"Did you in any way fabricate those photographs?" the reporter asked.

Another pause. "Of course not!" said Elsie.

"Are the fairies here now?" he asked.

Frances hesitated. "Yes," she said. Then a look of sadness passed over her face. "It's trodden round, everybody's been round. . . . No, I don't think so."

When she got home, Frances wrote the reporter a letter. "I'm sorry if I upset you by not taking you very seriously, but you so obviously thought we were a couple of confidence tricksters, and I've met so many people like you in the past." She admitted that she couldn't help enjoying his baffled expression as she answered his questions.

"I'm known as a woman who does not mince words . . . so you should feel a little grateful that I did not say to you, when you asked what I had to say and you didn't believe my story, 'Why the hell should I care what you think? My family and friends—I care for their opinion, but why should I care what a stranger thinks?' "

When a newspaper ran a story implying that Elsie and Frances were liars, Elsie was the one who responded. She wrote her letter by hand, in her big bold writing and eccentric spelling and punctuation. "(If people wish to believe in Fairies there is, No harm done.) And if people wish to think of us as a couple of practical jokers, or two solemn faced Yorkshire comedian's, thats alright too," she wrote. "But the word <u>liar</u> is a rough word for a true or untrue Fairy Story."

After that, an American hoax buster went after Elsie and Frances, but he couldn't prove anything.

Years and years went by, and nobody else could either, no matter how hard they tried.

Many people who looked at the quaint old photographs now could hardly believe that anybody had ever thought they were real.

But still . . . how could two such sweet little old ladies be *lying*?

TWENTY-ONE

Gorgeous and Precious Fairyland Places

It was Elsie who finally told.

It was because of her grandchildren, she said later—she didn't want them to think they had a "weirdy grandmother." So she told Glenn, who had never believed in the fairies anyway.

Glenn told Christine, and Christine didn't believe him. It couldn't be true!

Christine told Frances what Glenn had said. Then Frances was angry at Elsie, and Elsie was mad at Frances.

After that, nobody could agree exactly who told what to whom, and when.

But in time, Joe Cooper wrote that the secret of the fairies was out—they were paper cutouts. His articles appeared in a magazine called *The Unexplained: Mysteries of Mind Space & Time,* and they were announced on the cover alongside such stories as "Men from Mars" and "Whatever Happened to Dragons?" And he didn't say how he knew that the fairies were paper cutouts.

Still, Frances and Elsie were outraged.

"You're a traitor," Frances told him on the telephone. She slammed down the receiver.

Elsie wrote him in mock Yorkshire, "Tha's properly muckied tha' ticket wi' me!"

After that, both Elsie and Frances talked to reporters.

"Cottingley Fairies a Fake," said the headline in the *Times* of London on March 18, 1983. "Secrets of Two Famous Hoaxers," said a second *Times* article.

And that was that.

People believe what they read in the *Times,* and

there it was: Elsie and Frances were liars. The fairies were a hoax.

"I am sorry someone has stabbed all our fairies to death with a hatpin," Elsie told a reporter, but it was too late now.

Frances insisted that there *had* been fairies in the beck. She knew they were real! She knew that the last photograph was real! But no one really listened.

"No one has ever taken any notice of what I say," she wrote in her autobiography. She stopped writing it and put it away, unfinished.

But now, at last, neither Elsie nor Frances would ever have to lie about the fairies again.

In time, they made up and were friends again.

Frances's daughter and her grandchildren forgave her for not telling them about the cutouts. The real fairies were what mattered, and now Frances could tell them all about the little men without feeling guilty about lying. And Frances's daughter and grandchildren were proud of her. Christine was sure that

Frances, not Elsie, had taken the fairy bower photograph.

A real photograph, of real fairies.

Frances stood by the fairy bower photograph until the day she died. "Fairy Lady Dies with Her Secret," one newspaper said. But there wasn't any secret, not anymore. It was true that Frances had lied about the first four photographs. But that didn't mean the last one was a fake.

Frances had always known that she'd seen real fairies, there in the glen. Nothing could change that, ever.

Elsie lived the rest of her life in peace. She dug in her garden and told jokes and smiled her big, wide smile. She drew and painted steadily, as she had ever since she was a girl. She painted because she loved to, no matter what others thought of her art.

Which meant she was a real artist, and always had been.

She sometimes called the fairy pictures "photographs of figments of our imagination." And what is art, but a fine figment of the imagination? Art can be a painting. Or it can be a photograph. It can be a young girl, a waterfall, and a ring of fairies on a summer afternoon, captured forever by an artist's eye.

Elsie once wrote her autobiography, but the manuscript lay forgotten in a box. Then somehow, it disappeared. She once told somebody she'd only put in a couple of paragraphs about the fairies, anyway.

So . . . what did she really think about the long-held secret that changed her whole life? She never talked about it much. It was as though deep inside her was an oyster, crusted over with time, closed up tight.

Elsie did leave a little trail of clues, though, in a play she began but never finished. It's called *The Case of the Cottingley Fairies.*

ACT 1, SCENE 1

A figure slips through the closed curtains and stands in the spotlight at the front of the darkened stage. His name is Puck: he's the fairy from *A Midsummer Night's Dream.*

Puck jerks his thumb back toward the curtain and explains that behind it, a bunch of people are trying to pry open an oyster shell. It's sixty years old and crusted over with age. It's a great huge oyster—more than six feet wide.

Inside the oyster is one of two things.

"*(Either a pearl busting joke),*" Elsie wrote, or "*(A lustrous pearl of beauty) capable of whisking people's imaginations off to gorgeous and precious fairy land places.*"

The curtains swing open to reveal a group of men in shirtsleeves—they've taken off their ties and jackets—hammering away on the oyster. "*One man is standing aside with a pencil poised over a note book. Someone jibes at him for not helping, he says, 'I want to be the first to get it down on paper when the mystery comes unstuck,'*" Elsie wrote.

"*One hot and sweating worker yells, 'Hey! Did you hear that, chaps? This guy has been just standing there with a pencil in his hand while we have all been slogging our guts out,' to which the young writer replied:*

"'*The pen is mightier than the crow bar,' where-on the whole crowd of them down tools, put on their coats and disperse, one loud last remark from one of them saying, 'You can blooming well prise it open with your pencil then.' The writer now all alone with the giant shell, climbs up and sits down on top of it, then replaces his pen and writing pad to his pocket and then with his elbows on his knees he sits in sad contemplation.*

"Then to his astonishment, two wings expand from each side of the shell and away he floats."

Elsie's play ends here.

The oyster shell floats away.

But surely, now, the audience can tell that what's inside it is not a joke or a hoax. It's a fairy story with big, strong wings that can fly people's imaginations to gorgeous and fairyland places.

Now, as they sit in the darkened theater, maybe the audience can hear the low murmur of a stream in a hidden valley and the laughter of two young girls.

And maybe—if the air is very still and there isn't much rustling in the woods—they can just make out the faint, high piping of a gnome.

Acknowledgments

I first got the idea for *The Fairy Ring* when I was browsing in Common Good Books, a wonderful independent bookstore in St. Paul, Minnesota. At eye level, in the history section, I spotted a book called *The Coming of the Fairies,* by Sir Arthur Conan Doyle. I pulled it out, and there on the front cover was the picture of Elsie and the gnome.

For a long time, I've been interested in true stories with children as their heroes, and here was an *amazing* story. Who were these girls? What were they thinking?

Frances Griffith's autobiography, *Reflections on the Cottingley Fairies,* provides many clues. Whether you believe her little men were "real" or not, the fact that she saw them is not in doubt. I am grateful to her daughter, Christine, who published her mother's autobiography and dedicated it to Frances, "who always wanted the full story of the 'Cottingley Fairies' told."

The letters between Edward Gardner and the Wright family form the backbone of *The Fairy Ring.* Edward Gardner saved copies and passed them on to his son Leslie. Unfortunately, Leslie lived in a rather damp houseboat, but they're now well preserved in the Brotherton Collection at the University of Leeds. Elsie's letters to Leslie Gardner are in the West Yorkshire Archive Service, Bradford Central Library.

Most of all I would like to thank Elsie's son and daughter-in-law, Glenn and Lorna Hill, for all their gracious and good-humored help. They told me stories about Elsie and let me pore through their family photo albums, take down Elsie's watercolors from their walls to photograph them, and ransack their attic. Without them, this book would not have been possible.

My thanks also to Joe Cooper, whose long friendship with Frances and Elsie provided insights and firsthand accounts that would have been lost forever without his work. His book, *The Case of the Cottingley Fairies,* is dedicated to Frances and Elsie, "two amiable adventuresses" whose cutout fairies have not shaken Joe's belief in real ones.

Final thanks to Joe's family, to the archivists at the Brotherton Collection at the University of Leeds, to the many astute and patient readers who offered help and encouragement with drafts of this book, to my farsighted editor, Deb Wayshak, and to the good people of Cottingley today.

Source Notes

p. 10: "wide beaming smile": Griffiths, p. 6.

p. 13: "running water and the sun shining": Ibid., p. 10.

p. 15: "The best among the worst," and "the worst among the best": author interview with Glenn Hill.

pp. 23–24: "There is! I go up to see the fairies!" and "That's the end. You've started telling stories now!": Griffiths, p. 17.

p. 27: "Perhaps the advent . . . constant companion," "But there is no gainsaying . . . produced from plates," and "i.e. a room . . . has been excluded": Butcher, pp. 1 and 8–9.

pp. 28–29: "A steady pressure . . . shutter is released" and "jerky, sudden movement will seriously affect the ultimate picture": Ibid., p. 5.

p. 32: "There's one plate . . . take care of my camera" and "Now take care!": Griffiths, pp. 23 and 24.

p. 35: "sandwich papers": "There <u>Were</u> Fairies at the Bottom of the Garden," *Woman* magazine, October 1975, p. 43, Brotherton Collection.

p. 43: "Fairies—the pretty, pretty ones . . . not much I can say about them": Griffiths, p. 54.

p. 44: "Dear Joe . . . How are Teddy and Dolly?" and "Elsie and I . . . too hot for them there": Cooper, p. 192.

p. 47: "My little friend . . . amongst friends now": Griffiths, p. 39.

p. 54: "below the stairs" and "artistic ability": undated letter from Elsie Wright Hill to Virginia Chase, collection of Glenn Hill.

p. 58: "we all thought . . . nonsense!": author interview with Glenn Hill.

pp. 59–60: February 23, 1920, letter from Edward Gardner to Polly Wright, Brotherton Collection.

pp. 66–68: March 2, 1920, letter from Edward Gardner to Polly Wright, Brotherton Collection.

p. 70: "bathed in error and almost past praying for": Doyle, p. 16.

pp. 71–72: April 8, 1920, letter from Edward Gardner to Polly Wright, Brotherton Collection.

pp. 73–74: "I am myself convinced . . . let me know?": April 12, 1920, letter from Edward Gardner to Elsie Wright, Brotherton Collection.

p. 74: "She says I must thank you . . . lets her have the use of them now": April 15, 1920, letter from Polly Wright to Edward Gardner, Brotherton Collection.

p. 76: "We sat in a hut which had . . . the disappearance of our little visitors": Doyle, pp. 134–135.

p. 77: "What does it matter what anyone says of me. I have a good hide by this time": Lellenberg et al., p. 668.

p. 79: "psychic matters" and "I argued that we had . . . entirely beyond them": Doyle, p. 26.

p. 80: "They examined the plates . . . or other trick": Ibid., p. 33.

p. 84: "very shy and reserved indeed" and "They are of a mechanic's family . . . since babyhood": Ibid., p. 23.

p. 85: "Two children such as these . . . hey presto!!": Ibid., p. 24.

p. 85: "Everyone who saw them . . . understating the case": June 4, 1920, letter from Edward Gardner to Polly Wright, Brotherton Collection.

p. 87: June 14, 1920, letter from Elsie Wright to Edward Gardner, Brotherton Collection.

p. 88: June 30, 1920, letter from Arthur Conan Doyle to Elsie Wright, Brotherton Collection.

pp. 90–91: July 1, 1920, letter from Elsie Wright to Edward Gardner, Brotherton Collection.

pp. 91–92: "Yours sincerely, Arthur Conan Doyle, July 1920," *"The Lost World . . . Daily Gazette,"* "The Members of the Exploring Party," "The Swamp of the Pterodactyls," "Glade of the Iguanodons," and "The Central Lake": Brotherton Collection.

p. 93: "I have seen the very interesting photos . . . along with other material": June 30, 1920, letter from Arthur Conan Doyle to Arthur Wright, Brotherton Collection.

p. 93: "I heard him moan to my Mother, 'How could a brilliant man . . . such a thing?' ": undated letter from Elsie Wright Hill to Virginia Chase, collection of Glenn Hill.

p. 93: "our Elsie, and she at the bottom of her class": author interview with Glenn Hill.

p. 95: July 12, 1920, letter from Arthur Wright to Arthur Conan Doyle: Doyle, p. 34.

p. 96: "a shy, pretty girl of about sixteen": Gardner, p. 20.

p. 96: "She laughingly made me promise . . . so very long!" Doyle, p. 49.

p. 97: "I was glad of the opportunity . . . talking things over": Gardner, p. 21.

p. 97: "palest of green, pink, mauve" and "Much more in the wings . . . very pale to white": Doyle, p. 50.

p. 104: "If Elsie takes one flying . . . whole thing is so strange.": August 5, 1920, letter from Polly Wright to Edward Gardner, Brotherton Collection.

p. 105: "horribly uncomfortable" and "It wasn't a joke . . . got out of hand": Griffiths, p. 53.

p. 107: "I . . . left them to it": late August 1920 letter from Polly Wright to Edward Gardner, Brotherton Collection.

p. 108: "the deed was done": Griffiths, p. 54.

p. 108: "We wandered home . . . little men would be in my past": Ibid., pp. 55–56.

p. 110: "The weather was gloomy and we were gloomy" and "It was a hopeless task": Ibid., p. 56.

p. 112: "It's a queer one, we can't make it out": late August 1920 letter from Polly Wright to Edward Gardner, Brotherton Collection.

p. 112: "faded-out bits . . . might have been faces)": March 4, 1973, letter from Elsie Wright Hill to Leslie Gardner (Edward Gardner's son), West Yorkshire Archive Service, Bradford Central Library.

p. 112: "She didn't take one flying after all": late August 1920 letter from Polly Wright to Edward Gardner, Brotherton Collection.

p. 114: "I send just this line at once . . . about the fairies": November 25, 1920, letter from Edward Gardner to Elsie Wright, Brotherton Collection.

p. 114: "Fairies Photographed: An Epoch-Making Event Described by A. Conan Doyle" and "the two most astounding photographs ever published!": *Strand Magazine* 60, no. 360 (December 1920), pp. 463 and 462, Brotherton Collection.

pp. 114–116: "Should the incidents here narrated . . . examination and judgment" and "final and absolute proof": Doyle, p. 39.

p. 116: "Mr. Gardner, however, tested her . . . those in the photograph": Ibid., p. 57.

p. 116: "They threw cold water . . . paintings that hung in our house": undated letter from Elsie Wright Hill to the London *Daily Mail* in response to an article dated February 17, 1977, Brotherton Collection.

pp. 116–117: "There is an ornamental rim . . . let themselves go in the dance!": Doyle, p. 55.

pp. 119–120: "fed up," "Yes," "simply vanished into the air," "Yes," "If anybody else were there, the fairies would not come out," and "You don't understand": Ibid., pp. 67–69.

pp. 120–121: "transparent," "rather hard," and "You see, we were young then": Ibid., p. 70.

p. 121: "Do Fairies Exist? . . . Took the Snapshot" and "My mission to Yorkshire . . . that I failed": Ibid., pp. 60–61.

p. 23: "I would suggest to Miss Elsie . . . what the 'fairies' really are": London *Times,* January 5, 1921, Brotherton Collection.

p. 123: "I know children . . . have pulled one of them": Doyle, p. 88.

p. 124: "with your help in Cottingley . . . shall be justified everywhere": January 8, 1921, letter from Edward Gardner to Polly Wright, Brotherton Collection.

p. 125: "I am keeping them back . . . at the proper moment!": November 29, 1920, letter from Edward Gardner to Arthur Wright, Brother Collection.

p. 126: "The Evidence for Fairies . . . Photographs": *Strand Magazine* 61, no. 363 (March 1921), Brotherton Collection.

pp. 126–127: "fairy's bower" and "apparently considering . . . wonderful wings": Doyle, p. 103.

p. 127: "We have now succeeded . . . splendidly": Ibid., p. 101.

p. 127: "Never before, or otherwhere . . . been photographed!": Ibid., p. 103.

pp. 127–128: "Well, it would be interesting to have a few here in the classrooms" and "perfect fool": Griffiths, p. 60.

p. 128: "Thinking about fairies, then?": "There <u>Were</u> Fairies at the Bottom of the Garden," *Woman* magazine, October 1975, p. 43, Brotherton Collection.

p. 128: "This is what I hated for years . . . I didn't want to answer": Griffiths, pp. 60–61.

pp. 128–129: "mediumistic" and "subtle ectoplasmic or etheric material": Gardner, p. 25.

p. 133: "Our normal selves came to the surface": Griffiths, p. 65.

pp. 133–135: "Gnomes and Fairies . . . Elsie sees a small imp.": Doyle, pp. 108–115.

p. 135: "iridescent shimmering golden light": Ibid., p. 121.

p. 135: "When we two one step": Elsie Wright sketchbook,

collection of Glenn Hill; also reproduced in Cooper, photo insert following p. 112.

p. 139: "change in the girls": Doyle, p. 105.

p. 140: "When the last fairy pictures were taken . . . that was the end of it all": March 4, 1973, letter from Elsie Wright Hill to Leslie Gardner, West Yorkshire Archive Service, Bradford Central Library.

p. 141: "Briton in U.S. to Prove Fairies Exist": undated unidentified clipping, Brotherton Collection. "Champion of Elfs Struts His Stuff" and "A Bit of Britain's Gnome-land": undated *New York Evening Post* clipping, Brotherton Collection. "Really, Truly They're Fairies": undated *Los Angeles Examiner* clipping, Brotherton Collection.

p. 142: "like a landscape in the moon": Doyle, p. 125.

p. 144: "My husband always says . . . when he is laughing": April 24, 1971, letter from Elsie Wright Hill to Leslie Gardner, West Yorkshire Archive Service, Bradford Central Library.

p. 144: "Love, Frances": undated postcard, collection of Glenn Hill.

p. 144: "It was one of those things . . . always believed me": "There <u>Were</u> Fairies at the Bottom of the Garden," *Woman* magazine, October 1975, p. 43, Brotherton Collection.

p. 151: "Now I've told you, and I never want to hear about it again.": Griffiths, p. 74.

pp. 152–153: And one day, when Glenn was ten . . . And fairies were absolute nonsense: author interview with Glenn Hill.

p. 153: "She's never been skeptical . . . my grandchildren all the time": "There <u>Were</u> Fairies at the Bottom of the Garden," *Woman* magazine, October 1975, p. 43, Brotherton Collection.

p. 154: "a touch of 1920s dash about her" and "She has a dazzling smile . . . half of the county": "There <u>Were</u> Fairies at the Bottom of the Garden," *Woman* magazine, October 1975, p. 43, Brotherton Collection.

pp. 155–156: "Mind if I turn this on? I'm very interested in collecting data," "They say, jointly, calmly and lightly . . . pair of them get together," and "Once I was talking . . . fairies, do you, Elsie?": Cooper, pp. 123–124.

p. 156: "an air of mystery and gentleness and holding back something": Ibid., p. 125.

p. 157: "How big were the fairies? . . . No, I don't think so.": September 1976 Yorkshire Television (YTV) program, archives of the National Media Museum, Bradford, Yorkshire.

pp. 157–158: "I'm sorry if I upset you . . . in the past" and "I'm known as a woman . . . what a stranger thinks?": Griffiths, pp. 98–99.

p. 158: "(If people wish to believe in Fairies . . . true or untrue Fairy Story": undated letter from Elsie Wright Hill to the London *Daily Mail* in response to an article dated February 17, 1977, Brotherton Collection.

p. 160: "weirdy grandmother": February 17, 1989, letter from Elsie Wright Hill to Geoffrey Crawley, editor of the *British Journal of Photography,* archives of the National Media Museum, Bradford, Yorkshire. Elsie also told her son, Glenn Hill, that she wanted to reveal the secret out of concern for her grandchildren; author interview with Glenn Hill.

pp. 161–162: The sequence of how the secret was revealed is based on the accounts given in Griffiths and Cooper, on the dates of various newspaper and magazine articles of the time, and on author interviews with Glenn Hill.

p. 161: "Men from Mars" and "Whatever Happened to Dragons?": *The Unexplained: Mysteries of Mind Space & Time*, issues 20 and 21, Brotherton Collection.

p. 161: "You're a traitor" and "Tha's properly muckied tha' ticket wi' me!": Cooper, pp. 24 and 174.

p. 161: "Cottingley Fairies a Fake": London *Times*, March 18, 1983, p. 3. "Secrets of Two Famous Hoaxers": London *Times*, April 4, 1983, p. 3.

p. 162: "I am sorry someone has stabbed all our fairies to death with a hatpin": London *Times*, March 18, 1983, p. 3.

p. 162: "No one has ever taken any notice of what I say": Griffiths, p. 55.

p. 162: In time, they made up and were friends again: author interview with Glenn Hill.

p. 163: "Fairy Lady Dies with Her Secret": Norman Lebrecht, London *Sunday Times*, July 13, 1986.

pp. 163–164: The descriptions of Elsie Wright's later life are taken from her letters to Leslie Gardner, West Yorkshire Archive Service, Bradford Central Library. I learned about her autobiography and its fate from her son, Glenn Hill.

p. 163: "photographs of figments of our imagination": author interview with Glenn Hill.

pp. 165–166; "(Either a pearl busting joke) . . . precious fairy land places" and "One man is standing aside . . . each side of the shell and away he floats": Cooper, pp. 146–147.

Image Credits

pp. 12, 56, 82, 86,94, 138, and 145: illustrations and images courtesy of Glenn Hill, Glenn Hill personal collection; photographs © 2011 by Don Losure.

p. 31: Illustration from *Princess Mary's Gift Book*, p. 104

p. 37: "Alice and the Fairies," July 1917. Courtesy of Science and Society Library. Photographer Glenn Hill.

p. 42: "Iris and the Gnome," September 1917. Courtesy of Science and Society Library. Photographer Glenn Hill.

p. 65: "Come, Now a Roundel," 1908, by Arthur Rackham (1867–1939). Private Collection/© Chris Beetles, London, U.K./The Bridgeman Art Library.

p. 106: "Fairy Offering Flowers to Iris," August 1920. Courtesy of Science and Society Library. Photographer Glenn Hill.

p. 109: "Alice and Leaping Fairy," August 1920. Courtesy of Science and Society Library. Photographer Glenn Hill.

pp. 115 and 137: Photographs courtesy of the Brotherton Collection, Leeds University.

p. 147: "Fairy Sunbath Elves Etc.," August 1920. Courtesy of Science and Society Library. Photographer Glenn Hill.

Bibliography

PRINCIPAL SOURCES

Brotherton Collection, Leeds University Library. Papers and photographs relating to the Cottingley fairies, Handlist #170.

Butcher, W., & Sons Ltd. *Photography with a MIDG Magazine Camera.* (Instruction manual, undated.)

Cooper, Joe. *The Case of the Cottingley Fairies.* London: Pocket Books/Simon and Schuster, 1997.

Doyle, Arthur Conan. *The Coming of the Fairies.* New York: G. H. Doran, 1921.

Gardner, Edward L. *Fairies: A Book of Real Fairies.* London: Theosophical Publishing House, 1945.

Griffiths, Frances. *Reflections on the Cottingley Fairies: Frances Griffiths—In Her Own Words, with Additional Material by her Daughter Christine.* Belfast: JMJ Publications, 2009.

Lellenberg, Jon, Daniel Stashower, and Charles Foley, eds. *Arthur Conan Doyle: A Life in Letters.* New York: Penguin, 2007.

OTHER WORKS CONSULTED

Briggs, K. M. *The Fairies in English Tradition and Literature.* Chicago: University of Chicago Press, 1967.

Doyle, Charles Altamont. *The Doyle Diary: The Last Great Conan Doyle Mystery.* New York and London: Paddington Press Ltd., 1978.

Hodson, Geoffrey. *Fairies at Work and Play*. Wheaton, IL: Theosophical Publishing House, 1982.

Purkiss, Diane. *At the Bottom of the Garden: A Dark History of Fairies, Hobgoblins, and Other Troublesome Things*. New York: New York University Press, 2003.

Silver, Carole G. *Strange and Secret Peoples: Fairies and Victorian Consciousness*. New York: Oxford University Press, 1999.

Stashower, Daniel. *Teller of Tales: The Life of Arthur Conan Doyle*. New York: Holt, 1999.

Index

Note: Page numbers in *italic* type indicate images.

BBC, 153–154
brownies, 63, 64, 67, 134

Challenger, George E.,
    92, *94*
changelings, 63–64
Conan Doyle, Sir Arthur,
    75, 77–80, 84, 85,
    88–96, 98, 114,
    116–117, 123,
    126–127, 139
    The Coming of the Fairies,
    141–143, 150
    The Lost World, 89,
    91–93, *94,* 95, 144
Cooper, Joe, 155–156, 161
Cottingley, 5–10, 17,
    45–46, 47, 55, 79,
    81, 95, 98, 103–111,
    117, 145
    television crew in,
    155–156
    See also fairy photos

Elsie (Elsie Wright), 5, 6,
    9–10, 13–16, 18, 22,
    24, 25, 53–55, 63,
    72–74, 84–85, *86,*
    87–91, 95–99, 105,
    110, 113, 116–124,
    131–136, 139, 140
    adult life, 143–144,
    151–158, 163–166
    appearance of, 119,
    154, 155
    artistic talent, 10, *12,* 15,
    29–30, 55, *56,* 57,
    61, 81, *82,* 83, *106,*
    107–108, 116–117,
    135, 163–166
    child of, 151–153, 160
    hoax revealed, 160–164
    personality of, 15–16
    photos, *86, 106,* 118, 150
    unfinished play by,
    164–166
elves, 67, 134–135

fairies, 19–32, *31, 37,* 43,
    49, *56,* 97, 119–121

belief in, 58–63, 70,
  73, 75–78, 129–139,
  141–143, 150, 152,
  153, 162, 163
lore, 58, 63–64, 66,
  67, 134–135
"fairy bower" photo,
  111–112, 126–127,
  147, 148, 163
fairy photos, 15, 25, 26,
  32, 37, 42, 44, 53, 57,
  58, 61, 62, 66, 85,
  87, 106, 109, 136, 147
authenticity issue,
  71–74, 79–80, 88,
  93, 95–96, 114–116,
  124–126, 141,
  154–162
basis of, 29–30, 33–38,
  40–41, 55, 57, 61,
  105, 106, 107–108,
  109, 110, 124–126,
  144, 161, 162–163
Elsie's view of, 90, 91,
  163–164
end to, 140
Frances's view of, 105
glass plates of, 69–71, 80
growing fame of, 75, 78,
  89–90

hoax revealed, 160–164
lantern-slide shows of,
  75, 85, 141
site visits, 97, 129–139
Frances (Frances Griffith),
  3–18, 29–30, 36,
  38, 47–48, 88, 98,
  103–111, 113, 118–119,
  127–136, 140, 145
adult life, 144–146,
  148–151, 153–159
belief in fairies, 163
children of, 148–151,
  153, 162
discomfort of, 105,
  127–128
fairy sightings, 19–25,
  42, 111, 146, 148, 162
Gardner's view of,
  84–85, 128–130
hoax revealed, 160–163
photos, 35, 37, 39, 58,
  75, 109, 114, 117,
  145, 147

Gardner, Edward, 59–61,
  63, 66–75, 78–79,
  84, 87, 90–91, 95,
  103–107, 110, 111,
  116, 124

American tour, 141
article by, 114, *115*
beliefs, 70, 124–125,
   128–130, 150
"fairy bower" photo,
   127, 148
Wright family visit,
   96–99
gnomes, *42*, 96–98, 133,
   134, 143, 166
cutout photos, 40–41,
   42, 57, 67, 75, 96,
   111, 114, 147, 157
Great War, 4, 5, 10–11,
   38, 43, 45–46, 55,
   78, 146
Griffith, Frances. *See* Frances
Gunston, Mr., 54, 121–122

Hill, Frank, 143, 144, 151
Hill, Glenn, 151–153, 160
Hodson, Mr. and Mrs.,
   129–139, 157

India, 143, 151–152, 154
Ireland, 64, 66

lantern slides, 75, 85,
   87, 141
little men, 19–21, 36,

40–41, 47, 69, 108,
   111, 162
Lodge, Sir Oliver, 79
Lonsdale, Mr., 75–76
Los Angeles Examiner, 141

Malone, E. D., 92, *94*
Marjorie,136, *138*
mediums, 78, 128–129
Midsummer Night's Dream, A
   (Shakespeare), 55, 164

Rackham, Arthur, *56*, 57, *65*
Roxton, John, Lord, 92, *94*

séances, 78
Second World War, 146
Shakespeare, William, 55
Snowden, Ada, 38
spirit world, 77–78
Strand (magazine), 75, 114,
   115, 126
Summerlee, Professor,
   92, *94*

Theosophical Society,
   58–59, 61
Times of London, 123,
   161–162
Turvey, Mr., 75–76

water nymph, 133–134

Way, Cecil Wilfred, 144

Way, Christine, 148–151,
     153, 160, 162–163

Way, David, 149–150, 153

Wright, Arthur, 5, 9,
     15, 24, 29, 30, 32,
     34–35, 40–41, 44,
     45–46, 89, 90, 93,
     95–96, 108, 110, 111
   camera of, 26–29, 30,
     32, 34, 39–41
   teasing by, 14, 16,
     24–25, 30

Wright, Elsie. *See* Elsie

Wright, Polly, 5, 6–7, 24,
     29, 32, 36, 38, 39,
     57–61, 66–69, 71–72,
     74–75, 85, 96–97,
     104, 105, 107, 110,
     111–112, 151–152
   belief in fairy photos,
     124–125, 152
   grandson of, 151–152

The true story of a feral child and what happened when he was dragged into civilization.

"Beautiful. . . . Suffused with tender pathos."
— *The Wall Street Journal*

"A fascinating story . . . that becomes more intriguing as it unfolds." — *Publishers Weekly*

"A true story with obvious appeal to young readers. . . . This is a tale of finding humanity inside savagery." — *Booklist*

Available in hardcover and audio and as an e-book

Look for Mary Losure's next true tale from history

ISAAC
THE
ALCHEMIST

Meet Isaac.

Twelve years old, restless, angry, and living alone in an attic. He pores over a borrowed book called *The Mysteries of Nature and Art* and scribbles with his quill pen in a tiny notebook, writings that for all he knows no one will ever read. But they will. And the curious mind behind them will come to shape our understanding of the world around us.

Meet Isaac Newton.
Magician-scientist: alchemist.

COMING FALL 2015